Curriculum Bank

KEY STAGE ONE
SCOTTISH LEVELS A-B

INFORMATION TECHNOLOGY

ROB CROMPTON

Published by Scholastic Ltd,
Villiers House,
Clarendon Avenue,
Leamington Spa,
Warwickshire CV32 5PR
Text © Rob Crompton
© 1998 Scholastic Ltd
1 2 3 4 5 6 7 8 9 0   8 9 0 1 2 3 4 5 6 7

AUTHOR
ROB CROMPTON

EDITOR
JOEL LANE

ASSISTANT EDITOR
CLARE MILLER

SERIES DESIGNER
LYNNE JOESBURY

DESIGNER
SARAH ROCK

ILLUSTRATIONS
ANDY COOKE

COVER ILLUSTRATION
GAY STURROCK

SCOTTISH 5–14 LINKS
MARGARET SCOTT AND SUSAN GOW

Designed using Adobe Pagemaker

British Library Cataloguing-in-Publication Data
A catalogue record for this book is available from the
British Library.

ISBN 0-590-53782-2

Contents

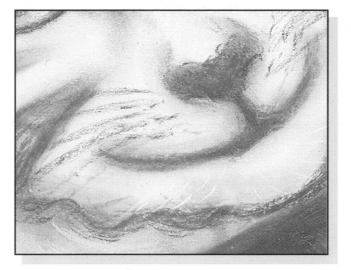

INFORMATION
TECHNOLOGY

ACKNOWLEDGEMENTS

The publishers gratefully acknowledge permission to reproduce the following copyright material:

© Logotron for the use of icons from *Revellation2*, published by Logotron, all trademarks acknowledged.
© RM plc for the use of icons from *Colour Magic*, published by RM plc, all trademarks acknowledged.
© SEMERC for the use of screens from the *My World* program, available from SEMERC, 1 Broadbent Road, Oldham OL1 4LB.

Introduction

Scholastic Curriculum Bank is a series for all primary teachers, providing an essential planning tool for devising comprehensive schemes of work as well as an easily accessible and varied bank of practical, classroom-tested activities with photocopiable resources.

Designed to help planning for and implementation of progression, differentiation and assessment, *Scholastic Curriculum Bank* offers a structured range of stimulating activities with clearly stated learning objectives that reflect the programmes of study, and detailed lesson plans that allow busy teachers to put ideas into practice with the minimum amount of preparation time. The photocopiable sheets that accompany many of the activities provide ways of integrating purposeful application of knowledge and skills, differentiation, assessment and record-keeping.

Opportunities for formative assessment are highlighted within the activities where appropriate, while separate summative assessment activities give guidelines for analysis and subsequent action. Ways of using information technology for different purposes and in different contexts, as a tool for communicating and handling information and as a means of investigating, are integrated into the activities where appropriate, and more explicit guidance is provided at the end of the book.

The series covers all the primary curriculum subjects, with separate books for Key Stages 1 and 2 or Scottish Levels A–B and C–E. It can be used as a flexible resource with any scheme, to fulfil National Curriculum and Scottish 5–14 requirements and to provide children with a variety of different learning experiences that will lead to effective acquisition of skills and knowledge.

INFORMATION TECHNOLOGY

SCHOLASTIC CURRICULUM BANK: INFORMATION TECHNOLOGY

The *Scholastic Curriculum Bank: Information Technology* books help teachers to plan a comprehensive and structured coverage of the primary IT curriculum and help pupils to develop the required skills, knowledge and understanding through activities that are usually linked to other curriculum areas. There is one book for Key Stage 1/Scottish Levels A–B and one for Key Stage 2/Scottish Levels C–E.

Bank of activities

Each book provides a range of activities that can be used in several different ways – to form a framework for a scheme of work; to add breadth and variety to an existing scheme or to supplement a particular subject activity. The activities are designed to be carried out in order, so that children develop IT skills progressively within a variety of curriculum contexts. The teaching of information technology is meant to support all curriculum subjects (apart from PE), and the majority of the activities have a strong subject context.

The IT skills developed in these activities will support work in a wide variety of subjects; cross-curricular links are outlined in the Overview Grid on pages 9–12. While children are using IT within the activities, they will be developing IT skills, knowledge and understanding. Some activities will develop their IT capability more efficiently than others. Teachers will need to be clear as to what particular IT skills can be developed through the various activities.

Discussion and demonstration

Part of the development of children's IT capability is their understanding of how IT is used in the outside world. Most of these activities have larger-scale applications in commerce or industry, and children need to be aware of this. Increasingly, IT systems around us are becoming so much a normal part of life that often we need to awaken children to their existence (the bar-code reader at the supermarket checkout, for example). Teachers need to ensure that children are aware of how their particular use of IT reflects similar activities beyond the classroom.

The nature of information technology

Through the wide range of activities that IT can be used for, children should realise how versatile a tool it is. IT can always offer quality output, although it may be some time before the children can achieve this. As with other curriculum areas, showing children examples of what can be achieved is helpful in the setting of standards. Children need to become skilled in the use of IT as a tool, and quality output will only follow the development of their IT skills.

Finally, children must come to realise that sometimes, technology will fail and let them down. This is bound to bring disappointment, but is part of the nature of the subject. We can learn to minimise the damage done by sudden failure (saving before printing, regular saving of files to back up our work), but we must never rely totally on this form of technology. There are many examples in the outside world where IT failure has caused undesirable results. This will also be reflected in your classroom from time to time!

Health and safety

There are EC regulations and guidelines for those who work with computers. However, it is unlikely that your children will be sitting in front of a computer for very long periods of time. Within the classroom context, there are a number of health and safety points you should follow:
▲ metal computer trolleys must be earthed;
▲ a computer should not be linked to the mains through a four-way extension lead beyond the computer trolley;
▲ children should not be responsible for plugging in electrical equipment.
These following points are recommended:
▲ adequate seating for your children so that their eyes are at the same level as the top of the monitor and their hands reach the keyboard comfortably;
▲ the monitor is not facing a window or source of bright light so causing uncomfortable glare or reflections;
▲ adequate space available around the computer for uncluttered mouse movements;
▲ the use of a mouse mat;
▲ all equipment is cleaned regularly; static electricity attracts dust particles and the equipment can become dirty very quickly, especially the monitor screen.

Lesson plans

Detailed lesson plans, under clear headings, are given for each activity and provide material for implementation in the classroom. The structure is as follows:

Activity title box

The information contained in the box at the beginning of each activity outlines the following key aspects:
▲ *Activity title and learning objective:* For each activity, a clearly-stated learning objective is given in bold italics. These learning objectives break down aspects of the programme of study into manageable teaching and learning chunks, and their purpose is to help teachers plan for progression. These objectives can be linked to the National Curriculum and Scottish 5–14 requirements by referring to the overview grid on pages 9–12. (The grid shows key areas of the PoS for each activity; but you will find that each activity covers numerous other aspects of the IT curriculum. Links to other subjects are also indicated.)
▲ *Class organisation/Likely duration:* The icons ♦♦ and ⏱ signpost the suggested group size for each activity and the approximate amount of time required to complete it. Time required at the computer is indicated separately from time

required for discussion/demonstration. Some activities are written to cover two or three sessions; you may also choose to extend other activities into more than one session.

▲ *Health and safety:* Where necessary, health and safety considerations are flagged by the icon ▲.

Previous skills/knowledge needed
This section indicates when it is necessary for the children to have acquired specific knowledge or skills prior to carrying out the activity. Other activities from the book that would provide suitable background experience are also suggested.

Key background information
The information in this section is intended to help the teacher to understand the IT concepts and ideas covered in each activity. It generally goes beyond the level of understanding of most children, but will help to give the teacher confidence to ask and answer questions and to guide the children in their investigations.

Language to be introduced
This section gives the key IT vocabulary which occurs naturally in the context of an activity. It also includes vocabulary for other subjects where appropriate.

Preparation
This section gives advice on any preparations needed for the activity. Details on setting up specific IT software or equipment are included as necessary.

Resources needed
All of the materials needed to carry out the activity are listed so that the teacher, or the pupils, can gather them together before the beginning of the teaching session. For many of the activities, a colour printer is preferable; but where it is essential, it is indicated in this section.

What to do
This section gives clear instructions, including suggestions for questions and discussion. It also highlights any problems that might arise and suggests how to solve them.

Suggestions(s) for extension/support
This section suggests ways of providing differentiation within the activity. In all cases, suggestions are provided as to how each activity can be modified for the less able or extended for the more able.

Assessment opportunities
Opportunities for formative assessment of the children's work, either during or after an activity, are highlighted.

Display ideas
Where appropriate, relevant and innovative display ideas are suggested and illustrated with examples.

Reference to photocopiable sheets
Where activities include photocopiable activity sheets, small reproductions of these are included in the lesson plans, together with notes on how they should be used. In order to avoid unnecessary repetition, sheets which are intended for use with more than one activity are only shown once.

Photocopiable sheets
Many of the activities are supported by photocopiable sheets for the teacher or children to use.

Cross-curricular links
The grid on page 144 shows those aspects of the activities which have a cross-curricular dimension, where IT might be used to support other curricular areas beyond the specific activities in the book.

INFORMATION TECHNOLOGY AT KEY STAGES 1 AND 2

Expectations in IT
There is a sense in which IT is not a subject in its own right, although, of course, it is recognised as a separate subject within the National Curriculum. The challenge for schools is to identify the relationship between IT and the other subject areas. The activities suggested in this book should not be seen in isolation but should always be carried out in the context of a particular subject. There is a requirement in each of the National Curriculum orders, except in PE, that IT must support children's learning. In terms of management, therefore, IT is best planned through subjects and moderated and evaluated using the IT Programme of Study and Level Descriptions.

The nature of IT
IT can be considered as a tool to support the development of knowledge and understanding of other subjects and, like any tool, it requires progressive acquisition of skills. Unlike other subjects with a long tradition in education, there is no generally accepted hierarchy of skill development within IT. However, some progression can be identified, and certain fundamental skills are recognised as a necessary base for further development. These ideas of progression have been incorporated into the sequence of activities in each chapter of this book. The activities should thus be undertaken in more or less the order in which they appear.

Classroom organisation and management

Throughout this book, it is assumed that access to computers is one per class, and therefore the activities will normally be completed over a period of days rather than within a single lesson. This, of course, has implications for classroom management in terms of organising a rota and monitoring children's time on the computer. Many of the activities start with a teacher demonstration. Depending on the size of the computer monitor, these initial discussions may be with the whole class or with smaller groups. This initial introduction provides useful opportunities for the teaching of IT skills and is an efficient use of curriculum time. After the context has been established and the tasks have been set, the children will normally carry out the activity in pairs or small groups.

The nature of IT is such that children are usually focused on the task in hand, but within a busy classroom you may need to establish a formal system of monitoring to ensure that all children complete the task within the agreed time.

Inevitably, while children are involved in IT activities, they may be missing out on other aspects of the curriculum. This is unavoidable, but through careful organisation of the pupil rota these effects should be minimised. Strategies should be considered to increase children's time on the computer. For example, children may be able to use a computer in another classroom which is currently not in use – perhaps during a PE lesson or class visit. In addition to reducing the time for all children to complete the task, this provides opportunities for the development of independent learning skills.

An essential part of good classroom management is the provision of a well-ordered and clean computer workstation. Of course, the children can be involved in maintaining the computer area. Indeed, some teachers appoint 'IT consultants' who provide first-call practical support for simple technical problems and general help for the less confident children.

Monitoring and assessment

It is important that all children have equal access to the variety of IT activities required by the programme of study. A useful way of monitoring in the classroom is to involve children in the process. For example, for each activity provide a sheet posted beside the workstation on which children enter the date and period of time spent on the computer. You may prefer to use a booklet for this purpose. At a glance, you can see which children have had access to the computer and for how long.

There is a wider level of monitoring, as seen in the school's yearly or termly curriculum overview. Within this there should be seen opportunities to offer children the full range of IT activities. You need to ensure that the activities you plan into your curriculum reflect the expectations laid out in the long-term planning.

Careful monitoring provides information for assessment. Many of the activities in this book identify opportunities for gathering this. Whereas the assessment of the children's finished product after an activity is relatively straightforward, assessing the process of making it is more complex.

If children maintain individual records of achievement, these provide a useful basis for focused discussion from which the level of their knowledge and understanding can be established. At appropriate points, the level descriptions for IT can then be used to judge the 'best fit' for each child. This process is essential in ensuring progression. Together with day-to-day informal assessment, this can feed into subsequent class and whole-school planning.

IT at home

The pace of change in IT gives rise to particular challenges. Unlike other subjects in the National Curriculum, the rapid development of IT is having a huge impact on most aspects of everyday life. The increase in the number of home computers has important implications for education. Many children have a high level of technical skill, and sometimes teachers feel they are not able to capitalise on this. However, teachers have an important role in (a) making sure that children's knowledge and understanding is extended, and (b) exploiting such expertise for the benefit of other children.

The skills that children have are often highly software-specific, and it is important to ensure their range of expertise is extended. Where children are used as classroom 'IT consultants', they need careful induction into the role to ensure that the support they provide enables less confident children to develop their own independent skills.

Resources

The activities within this book have been designed around the computers and software commonly found in schools. Most of them require only a basic hardware system. None of the activities are dependent on any specific computer system. In order to rationalise the management of IT across the curriculum, a small and carefully selected 'toolbox' of programs is recommended. This enables teachers to develop an in-depth knowledge of particular software and helps children to progress smoothly within a familiar software context.

INFORMATION
TECHNOLOGY

Overview grid

Learning objective	Title	PoS/AO	Subject links	Content/type of activity	Page
Chapter 1: Communicating information					
To understand that a computer can print text. To develop skills in the use of a touch-sensitive keyboard.	Winter words	1.1a; 1.2a/ Level A	English: Writing 3.1a, 3.2a	Class activity led by the teacher. Introducing the touch-sensitive keyboard.	14
To develop familiarity with a touch-sensitive keyboard. To know that pictures on an overlay can represent text on a word processor file. To develop skill in using the enter/return and delete keys.	Ice breaker	1.1a; 1.2a/ Level A	English: Writing 2.2e, 3.1a, 3.2a	Paired activity using the touch-sensitive keyboard to arrange events in sequence and produce text on screen.	16
To develop keyboard skills: finding correct keys to enter text and deleting mistakes.	This is me!	1.1a; 1.2a/ Level A	English: Writing 3.1a, 3.2a	Pairs producing individual tray/bedroom labels using a word processing program.	18
To choose different fonts and text sizes. To centre and colour text. To develop keyboard skills further.	Topical titles	1.1a; 1.2a/ Level B	English: Writing 3.1a, 3.2a	Pairs producing individual title pages for a topic folder using a word processing program.	19
To insert and delete text on a computer.	Filling the gaps	1.1a; 1.2a/ Level B	English: Reading 2.2b	Pairs completing cloze texts on a screen provided by the teacher.	21
To become more familiar with the centreing facility of a word processor. To use IT for a purpose in a realistic context.	What's on the menu?	1.1a, b, c; 1.2a/ Level B	English: Writing 3.1a, 3.2a	Pairs producing 'My favourite meal' menus using a word processing program.	22
To position words and numbers on a computer screen using the tab facility.	Chef's special	1.1a, b, c; 1.2a/ Level B	English: Writing 3.1a, 3.2a; D & T 1.1a, 1.2a	Pairs producing a recipe relating to cooking activities using a word processing program.	24
To develop greater familiarity with a touch-sensitive keyboard. To reinforce the skills of using the enter/return and delete keys.	Pen portraits	1.1a, b, c; 1.2a/ Level A	English: Writing 3.1a, 3.2a	Pairs writing descriptions of themselves and producing text from a touch-sensitive keyboard.	25
To develop word-processing skills related to letter writing, using a conventional layout. To use the justify facility for left and right alignment.	Dear Sir	1.1a, b; 1.2a/ Level B	English: Writing 3.1a, 3.2a, b, c, d, 3.3a	Pairs producing, for example, individual letters to a classroom helper, a relative or a sick child, using a word processing program.	28
To insert a picture into a page of text.	How it looks	1.1a; 1.2a/ Level B	English: Writing 3.1a, 3.2a, b, c, d, 3.3a; Art 2a, b, 3	Pairs or small groups writing a brief response to a picture, piece of music or visit. Using clip art or products from a graphics package to enhance descriptions.	30
To practise drafting and redrafting text using a word processor.	Short and sweet	1.1a; 1.2a/ Level B	English: Speaking and Listening 1.1a, b, c, 1.2 a, b, Writing 3.1a, b, c, 3.2a, b, c, d, 3.3a	Groups working together to produce a short story or poem using a word processing program.	31
To understand the potential of a word processor as a tool for creative writing.	The words that count	1.1a; 1.2a/ Level B	English: Writing 3.1a, 3.2a, b, c, d, 3.3a	Pairs or small groups using prompt words to write a poem using a word processing program.	33
To develop familiarity with the uses of a touch-sensitive keyboard. To practise the keyboard skills of entering text using the enter/return and delete keys.	Who's who	1.1a; 1.2a/ Level A	English:Writing 3.1a, 3.2a, b, c, d, 3.3a	Small groups collecting information and writing factual descriptions for use with a touch-sensitive keyboard.	34
To further understand the potential of the word processor as a tool for creative writing. To practise 'copy and paste'.	Wax lyrical	1.1a; 1,2a/ Level B	English: Writing 3.1a, b, c, 3.2a, b	Pairs writing lyrics for their own musical compositions using a word processing program.	36
To develop confidence in word-processing skills and desktop publishing skills. To use IT for a real purpose: producing a newsletter or newspaper for actual readers.	News desk	1.1a; 1.2a/ Level B	English: Writing 3.1a, b, c, 3.2a, b, c, d, 3.3a; Speaking and Listening 1.1a, b, c, 1.2a, b	Whole-class activity, directed by the teacher. Groups and individuals working in items for a class newsletter using a word processing program, clip art and a graphics program.	37

Learning objective	Title	PoS/AO	Subject links	Content/type of activity	Page
To introduce painting with coloured light on the computer screen. To practise mouse control. To introduce the 'fill' facility.	Take a pencil for a walk	1.1a; 1.2a/ Level B	Art 1, 2c, 4b, d	Pairs producing individual images using a graphics program.	39
To introduce the use of 'stamps'. To refine the skills of 'dragging and dropping'.	Stamp it out	1.1a; 1.2a/ Level B	Art 1, 2c, 4b, d	Pairs experimenting with the stamp facility within a graphics program.	41
To introduce the autoshape facility. To practise using 'fill'.	Get into shape	1.1a; 1.2a/ Level A	Art 1, 2c, 4b, d, 7e, 9b, d	Pairs working from a Mondrian stimulus to produce a shared computer image.	42
To introduce and practise 'cut and paste' techniques. To understand and appreciate the power of the computer to generate graphic images.	Look, no scissors!	1.1a; 1.2a/ Level B	Art 1, 2c, 4b, d	Pairs working from a William Morris stimulus to produce repeat patterns using a graphics program.	44
To further understand and appreciate the power of the computer to generate graphic images. To practise using the 'fill' tool. To practise retrieving a file. To practise printing out independently.	Colour swops	1.1a; 1.2a/ Level B	Art 1, 2c, 4b, d	Pairs developing previous work by making multiple printouts of computer images using different colours, or shades of the same colour.	46
To develop mouse skills further. To select, resize and rotate shapes using the 'autoshape' facility.	Planet of the shapes	1.2a; 1.2a/ Level B	Art 1, 2c, 4b, d	Pairs working together to produce a 'space' picture from regular shapes within a graphics program.	47
To develop mouse skills further. To select, resize and 'paste' shapes. To combine autoshapes with freehand work, judging which is more appropriate. To load a program, save and print out with increasing independence.	Underwater	1.1a; 1.2a/ Level B	Art 1, 2c, 4a, b, c, 8f, 9b, d	Pairs working together to produce an 'underwater' picture from regular shapes within a graphics program.	48
To develop mouse skills further. To develop skills in freehand drawing using painting tools. To load a program, save and print out with increasing independence.	Light and shade	1.1a; 1.2a/ Level B	Art 1, 2b, 4a, b, 8a, d, f, 9b, d	Pairs working with a graphics program to produce silhouettes of individual faces, following stimulus from shadow graphs and miniatures.	50
To be introduced to the 'paint spray' facility and practise using it.	Spray that again!	1.1a; 1.2a/ Level B	Art 1, 2b, 4a, b, 8a, d, f, 9b, d	Pairs using the paint spray facility in a graphics program to make subtle changes to colour, shade and tone.	51
To practise screen painting techniques in the context of representational art. To understand the advantages and disadvantages of using a computer rather than conventional media.	Fearful symmetry	1.1a; 1.2a/ Level B	Music 1a, 2g	Pairs producing individual pictures using a graphics program.	53
To extend screen painting techniques in the context of representational art. To understand further the advantages and disadvantages of using a computer rather than conventional media. To be introduced to 'clip art' and practise saving and retrieving images on disk.	Yes, that's me with the parachute	1.1a; 1.2a/ Level B	Music 1a, 2a, b, g	Pairs producing individual pictures of 'What I like doing', using a graphics program.	54
To be introduced to the idea of representing musical phrases by pictures. To know the techniques for playing individual phrases and creating a musical sequence (using the 'drag and drop' technique).	Three blind mice	1.1a; 1.2a/ Level B	Music 1a, 2a, b, d, g, 5b, f, h	Teacher leading class or group activity using a music program. Rearranging jumbled musical phrases to produce the tune 'Three Blind Mice'.	56
To practise the techniques for playing individual phrases, and for creating a musical sequence using a the 'drag and drop' technique.	The teddy bears' picnic	1.1a; 1.2a/ Level B	Music 1a, 2a, b, d, g, 5b, f, h	Teacher leading class or group activity using a music program. Children picking out musical phrases that sound like beginnings, middles or ends of tunes.	57

Learning objective	Title	PoS/AO	Subject links	Content/type of activity	Page
To practise further the techniques for playing individual phrases and for creating a musical sequence.	If you're happy and you know it	1.1a; 1.2a/ *Level B*	Music 1a, 2a, b, d, g, 5b, f, h	Pairs or threes working on an 'upbeat' composition, using given musical phrases within a music program.	58
To practise further the techniques for playing individual phrases and for creating a musical sequence. To know how to change the speed of a tune.	From major to minor	1.1a; 1.2a/ *Level B*	Music 1a, 2a, b, d, g, 5b, f, h	Pairs or threes working on a 'low-key' composition, using given musical phrases within a music program.	60
To develop an understanding of how computers are integrated into many forms of music. To use the computer alongside conventional instruments for performing compositions.	Join the band	1.1a, b; 1.2a/ *Level B*	Music 1a, 2a, b, d, g, 5b, f, h	Groups playing back their computer compositions and accompanying them using a variety of non-pitched percussion instruments.	61

Chapter 2: Handling information

Learning objective	Title	PoS/AO	Subject links	Content/type of activity	Page
To know how a computer can be used to collect, sort and display information. To begin to interpret data.	Six snakes, four ferrets	1a, b, c; 1.2a, b, c/ *Level B*	Maths 1.3d, 2.1f, 2.5a, b	Teacher leading activity with the whole class, collecting information about pets and displaying it as bar graphs and pie charts.	64
To know how a computer can be used to collect, sort and display information. To develop further ability to interpret data.	Traffic jam	1a, b, c; 1.2a, b, c/ *Level B*	Maths 1.3d, 2.1f, 2.5a, b; Geography 1a, b, 2, 3b, 4, 6	Teacher leading activity with the whole class, collecting and displaying data about traffic flow.	65
To develop independence in collecting data and using a computer to display it as a bar chart or pie chart.	Shampoo and set	1a, b, c; 1.2a, b, c/ *Level B*	Maths 1.3d, 2.1f, 2.5a, b	Teacher leading activity with the whole class and paired activities, collecting and displaying data on hair colour.	67
To practise collecting data and recording it on data collection sheets. To understand the need for accuracy. To see the relevance of information handling to everyday life. To work co-operatively.	Down at heel	1a, b, c; 1.2a, b, c/ *Level B*	Maths 1.3d, 2.1f, 2.5a, b; Science 0, 1c, d, 1.2c, 1.3b, c, d, 2.4a	Children collecting data on shoe sizes and entering data into a prepared database.	69
To collect numerical data and record it under class intervals.	Up the wooden hill	1a, b, c; 1.2a, b, c/ *Level B*	Maths 1.3d, 2.1f, 2.5a, b	Whole-class activity. Children collect data about bedtimes and teacher enters data into database.	70
To choose an appropriate mode of display for data. To practise selecting from menu options and loading data files. To provide opportunities for teacher assessment of information-handling skills.	Charting success	1a, b, c; 1.2a, b, c/ *Level B*	Maths 1.3d, 2.1f, 2.5a, b	Pairs choosing to display existing information as bar graphs, pie charts and so on.	72
To be introduced to the use of a CD-ROM for information handling.	Discovery	1a, b, c; 1.2a, b, c/ *Level B*	Various possibilities	Groups of three using a CD-ROM to find and record information.	73
To practise the use of a CD-ROM for information handling. To copy and paste from a CD-ROM to a word processor.	CD snaps	1a, b, c; 1.2a, b, c/ *Level B*	Various possibilities	Groups of three using a CD ROM to find information, cutting text and pictures from the CD-ROM and pasting them into a word processor.	75
To practise making and collecting accurate observations. To enter the data into a simple spreadsheet.	Weather watch	1a, b, c; 1.2a, b, c/ *Level B*	Maths 1.3d, 2.1f, 2.5a, b; Geography 5c	Ongoing daily activity. Children take turns to enter data about weather into a spreadsheet set up by the teacher.	77
To practise making and collecting accurate observations. To enter the data into a simple spreadsheet. To sort the data using particular criteria.	How does it feel?	1a, b, c; 1.2a, b, c/ *Level B*	Maths 1.3d, 2.1f, 2.5a, b; Science 3.1a, b, c	Activity related to study of materials in science. Pairs enter information into a prepared spreadsheet and sort.	79

Chapter 3: Modelling and control

Learning objective	Title	PoS/AO	Subject links	Content/type of activity	Page
To model a real-life process using modelling software. To develop keyboard skills.	The bear essentials	1.3b/ *Level B*	Science 2.2a; Geography 5c	Children working in pairs to dress a teddy bear on the computer screen.	84
To model a real-life process using a computer program. To develop keyboard skills further. To practise printing out work.	That's life!	1.3b/ *Level B*	Science 2.1b	Children working in pairs to arrange a life cycle sequence in the correct order on the computer screen.	85

INFORMATION
TECHNOLOGY

Learning objective	Title	PoS/AO	Subject links	Content/type of activity	Page
To know that switches control everyday devices.	Switched on	1.1b, c; 1.3a/ *Level B*	Science 4.1a, c	Individual activity around school and at home. Searching for devices with switches that can be turned on/off.	86
To know that switches are often calibrated. To know that '1' usually signifies low and '10' usually signifies high.	Turn it up	1.1b, c; 1.3a/ *Level A*	Science 4.1a, c	Individual activity around school and at home. Searching for switches (including dials) with numbers.	88
To know that computer icons are often used to represent functions.	In the picture	1.1b, c; 1.3a/ *Level A*	Science 4.1a, c	Individual activity around school and at home. Searching for devices with icons.	89
To know that switches can be hidden and can respond to movement or changes in pressure, light or temperature.	Secret switches	1.1b,c, 1.3a/ *Level B*	Science 0.2a 4.1a, c	Teacher leading whole-class activity. Supermarket visit to identify electronic switches.	91
To understand the concept of moving forward or back and turning left or right in relation to a given position. To know that, in basic control technology activities, *right/left 1* indicates a turn of one right angle.	Direct a friend	1.3b/ *Level B*	Maths 3.3a, b	Teacher leading whole-class activity. Pairs give instructions to each other, writing the sequence down using their own symbols or shorthand.	92
To develop the concept of moving forward or back and turning left or right in relation to a given position. To record commands using arrow symbols.	Direct a toy	1.3b/ *Level B*	Maths 3.3a, b	Group activity with support. Children move a toy around, recording the sequence using arrow symbols.	94
To reinforce the concept of moving forward or back and turning left or right in relation to a given position. To practise recording commands using arrow symbols. To be introduced to programming a floor robot using a sequence of commands.	Robot walk	1.1a; 1.3b/ *Level B*	Maths 3.1b, 3.3a, b	Group activity with support. Children program a floor turtle using familiar commands.	96
To practise programming a floor or table robot.	Slalom	1.1a; 1.3b/ *Level A*	Maths 3.1b, 3.3a, b	Group activity with support. Children program a floor turtle to follow a specific route.	98
To practise more flexible programming of a floor robot.	Obstacle course	1.1a; 1.3b/ *Level B*	Maths 3.1b, 3.3a, b	Group activity with support. Children program a floor turtle to negotiate obstacles.	99
To practise programming a floor or table robot. To use the 'Wait' command.	Robopostman	1.1a; 1.3b/ *Level A*	Maths 3.1b, 3.2a, b	Group activity with support. Programming a floor turtle to *wait* for a number of seconds.	100
To program a floor or table robot using the 'Repeat' command. To use a robot with the drawing device attached.	Square dance	1.1a; 1.3b/ *Level B*	Maths 3.1b, 3.2a, b	Group activity with support. Programming a floor turtle to travel through a square using the *Repeat 4* command. Recording the journey using the turtle's pen facility.	102
To program a floor or table robot using procedures.	Procedures	1.1a; 1.3b/ *Level B*	Maths 3.1b, 3.2a, b	Paired activity. Following introduction by the teacher, children program a floor turtle using procedures.	103
To program a screen turtle using commands familiar from work with floor robots.	Turn turtle	1.1a; 1.3b/ *Level B*	Maths 3.1b, 3.2a, b	Paired activity using a screen Logo program. Following demonstration by the teacher, children give each other commands to execute on screen.	105
To build procedures using the 'Repeat' command. To save procedures.	Screen square	1.1a; 1.3b/ *Level B*	Maths 3.1b, 3.2a, b	Paired activity with support. Following demonstration by the teacher, children draw squares of various sizes on the screen using the *Repeat 4* command and save the procedures.	106

Entries given in italics refer to the Scottish 5–14 Guidelines for Information Technology within Environmental Studies.

INFORMATION TECHNOLOGY

Communicating information

The activities in this section of the book give children opportunities to explore the many facilities that IT offers for communicating information. The three main forms in which information can be communicated are text, sound and images.

Software that allows text to be manipulated – word processing and desktop publishing – is commonplace in schools; it offers children a cross-curricular resource which they can use to communicate information about any topic or aspect of their experience. Whenever possible, children should write at the screen rather than copy previously written material onto a word processor.

Communication by pictures or graphics is a highly significant IT facility. IT also allows us to predict appearances, and thus to see what things will look like before they are made. Painting with light on the computer screen requires quite different skills from those used in conventional art. As well as providing an additional medium within the art curriculum, painting or drawing software can be used to enhance and illustrate any area of school work.

Communicating by sound usually takes the form of musical composition and performance using the computer. In order to improve the quality and variety of the sound, the computer can often be linked to an electronic keyboard. The use of music software offers opportunities for children to compose and record their own tunes without needing to use standard notation.

INFORMATION
TECHNOLOGY

WINTER WORDS

To understand that a computer can print text. To develop skills in the use of a touch-sensitive keyboard.

†† *Whole-class discussion and activity.*

🕐 *15 minutes discussion time; 30 minutes computer time.*

Key background information

Entering and editing text on a word processor is one of the most common computer-based activities. However, using the standard 'qwerty' keyboard requires some knowledge of the layout of the letters, as well as English skills such as spelling. This activity allows children who are still developing basic literacy and keyboard skills to gain an understanding of how the computer can be used for writing.

About twenty years ago, a touch-sensitive pad was developed in order to help disabled people interact with a computer. For example, where someone had insufficient fine motor control to locate and press the individual keys on a conventional keyboard, he/she could press words on the pad with a hand or an elbow and produce text on the screen. Subsequently, several other uses were found for this type of pad – for example, many hotels and garages use it: instead of entering the price of a drink or a spare part for a car, the operator presses a picture of the item and the price appears on the till display.

The educational potential of this method of interaction with the computer was quickly recognised. Although they were first used with very young children and children with special needs, these keyboards are currently used across the primary and secondary phases for a variety of complex

applications including data handling and music. The first touch keyboards for educational use were supplied by a company called 'Computer Concepts'; as a result, the generic term for them became *concept keyboards*.

The concept keyboard consists of a grid of touch-sensitive cells (which do not need to be pressed, only touched). Sample files and software to run the system are supplied with the keyboard, which plugs into one of the sockets or 'ports' in the back of the computer. Most educational word processing software is designed to accept input from a concept keyboard as well as the standard keyboard. Both can be used at the same time.

The exact method of operation depends on the computer system and word processing software being used. Common to all methods is the use of an *overlay* (a set of specific images or words). This is placed on top of the concept keyboard, and the file associated with the particular overlay is linked into the system.

It is easy to produce your own concept keyboard overlays for a current topic. For example, an overlay (see Figure 1) which contained a bank of words connected with winter might be linked to a file with the name Winterword. This overlay also has cells which allow children to operate the *delete* and *return* functions using the concept keyboard. With this overlay, the children would be able to produce a piece of writing containing words they had typed into a standard keyboard and words they had selected by pressing the appropriate area on the concept keyboard.

INFORMATION TECHNOLOGY

Figure 1

gloves	icicles	cold	tingling
February	dull	winter	snug in bed
umbrella	white	grey	**DELETE**
frozen	hibernating	grit	**RETURN**

In a more recent extension of this idea, a bank of words (and sometimes associated pictures) appears at the bottom of the computer screen. Children select the required words by clicking on them with the mouse, and the words appear beside the cursor on the main screen. This is more flexible than a concept keyboard, since the word bank can be added to at any time. However, the concept keyboard itself can be used in more varied ways: the overlays can be produced in a variety of forms, such as a display of colour photographs.

Language to be introduced
Overlay.

Resources needed
A computer with a word processing program, a touch-sensitive keyboard linked to the computer, an overlay with an associated file.

Preparation
Make sure you are familiar with the system beforehand.

Produce a word bank overlay containing words related to a current topic. Further examples are shown in Figure 2. The associated file will be created automatically as you enter the words. Set up the word processor-concept keyboard link.

What to do
Within the context of work on the seasons (or any other suitable aspect of the current topic), discuss how the children might describe winter. Prompt them to suggest appropriate words and phrases. Ask them to think about winter with a view to writing a poem, perhaps drawing pictures to consolidate their ideas. Make a note of their suggestions and, before the next session, create an overlay containing the words and phrases they have suggested.

Gather the children around the computer and key in 'Winter is' several times, starting a new line each time. Use a large font so that everyone can see the text clearly.

Figure 2: Examples of overlays to support writing

Picnic

ice cream	car	cut		
lemonade	hot	brother		
swim	in	picnic	Delete	Return
mum	dad	money		

Phrase

mum	dad	television		am	is	was	play
home	house			were	will	can	go
shop	day			have	has	come	went
car	park			saw	got	get	watch
I	my	you	our	the	like		
it	we	him	some	a	with		
not	out	in	to	no	like		
and	yes						

Remind the children of the previous discussion about winter, and show them the overlay you have made which contains their suggestions. Tell them that you would like their help in writing a poem.

Demonstrate how pressing a word on the concept keyboard produces the text on the screen, and invite volunteers to complete the first line of the poem by adding a word or phrase to 'Winter is'. Continue in this way until all the lines are complete. Invite the children to suggest a different beginning to the line, such as 'Icicles are', and ask for further volunteers to select words from the concept keyboard. Make a point of suggesting words that are not on the overlay and typing these in directly, showing how the two methods of entering text can be used as alternatives.

When the poem is completed to the children's satisfaction, print it out and duplicate a copy for each child.

Suggestion(s) for extension

More confident children could try writing their own poem, using the same overlay.

Suggestion(s) for support

Make sure that less confident children are included in the process of writing the class poem by inviting their contributions.

Assessment opportunities

As the children enter words and phrases, ask them to talk through the process and note their level of understanding.

Display ideas

The completed poem could be included in a class anthology. It could be enlarged and displayed with other creative work.

ICE BREAKER

*To develop familiarity with a touch-sensitive keyboard. To know that pictures on an overlay can represent text on a word processor file. To develop skill in using the **enter/return** and **delete** keys.*

†† *Whole-class discussion; paired activity.*

🕐 *20 minutes discussion/demonstration time; 10 minutes computer time.*

⚠ *Emphasise the dangers of playing on ice.*

Previous skills/knowledge needed

The children need to have been introduced to the concept keyboard (see 'Winter words' on page 14), and to know that pressing such a keyboard can produce text on a computer screen.

Figure 3

INFORMATION TECHNOLOGY

Key background information

The 'Winter words' activity on page 14 explains the ideas of a concept keyboard and an overlay. An overlay does not need to contain text. However, if pictures are used on the overlay, pressing a picture will cause text to appear on the screen rather than the picture itself. (There are rare exceptions to this.)

The example used in this activity concerns playing on ice, but other sequences such as baking cakes or getting dressed would be just as appropriate. A sentence for each picture can be entered into the overlay file (the exact method will depend on the particular software being used). In the sample overlay shown in Figure 3, the first picture in the sequence (bottom left) could be linked to 'Jenny and her friends were playing near the pond.' The associated file will be created automatically as you enter the words.

Language to be introduced

Sequence.

Resources needed

A computer with a word processing program, a touch-sensitive keyboard linked to the computer, an overlay with an associated file.

Preparation

Make sure you are familiar with the system beforehand. Produce an overlay (similar to that shown in Figure 3) with pictures which need to be put into the correct sequence. Enter the linked text, using vocabulary appropriate for the class. Set up the word processor-concept keyboard link.

What to do

Within an appropriate context (such as work on winter or safety), show the children the overlay and ask them whether they think the pictures are in the correct order. Ask them to suggest which picture should come first, and build up the story with them. Remind them of their previous work with the concept keyboard; now introduce the idea of pictures being used to generate text on the screen. Emphasise that pressing the picture will produce text rather than the picture itself. Demonstrate this by pressing the first picture in the sequence and producing the associated sentence on the screen. Press some more pictures at random until the children have grasped the idea. Demonstrate how the *enter/ return* key can be used to start a new line, and how the *delete* key can be used to correct mistakes.

Organise the children into pairs and establish a rota for using the computer. Set the task, which is for each pair to produce the story on screen using the sentences in the correct order.

Suggestion(s) for extension

More confident children could be encouraged to add more text to the basic story, using the standard keyboard.

Suggestion(s) for support

Provide adult support as children start the task, gradually reducing this as appropriate.

Assessment opportunities

Look for children using the *enter/return* and *delete* keys,

INFORMATION TECHNOLOGY

and note their level of accuracy and confidence.

Display ideas

When the children have completed the task, the pictures and associated sentences could be cut out from the children's printouts and stuck into their books or onto a sheet of paper.

THIS IS ME!

To develop keyboard skills: finding correct keys to enter text and deleting mistakes.

†† *Whole-class discussion; paired activity.*

🕐 *20 minutes discussion/demonstration time; 10 minutes computer time.*

Previous skills/knowledge needed

The children need to know how to spell their names, starting with a capital letter.

Key background information

Developing word-processing skills is necessary for all children at Key Stage 1. Within the limited time that is usually available for individual computer work, a short activity is often more appropriate than asking the child to key in a long passage of text. This activity includes finding the appropriate letter keys and deleting mistakes. It would be an appropriate activity to try at the beginning of a school year or term.

Language to be introduced

Capital letter, centre, font, space, back space, enter, delete.

Preparation

Set up a page on the computer screen beforehand. Select an appropriate font, type size and colour, but do not enter any text at this stage. A font size of 40 points would be suitable.

Resources needed

A computer with a word processing program, a colour printer, scissors and adhesive (teacher only).

What to do

Talk to the children about the need for some things in the classroom – such as their trays – to be clearly labelled. If they do not have individual trays, the activity could focus on making a label for each child's bedroom door.

Demonstrate how to enter your own name on the computer. Emphasise the use of a capital letter for the first letter, and show how this can be done by holding the shift key down while typing.

Explain to the children how you selected the size and colour of the letters. Introduce the word 'font'. Make a mistake in your typing and show them how to correct it using the 'back space' key. If a child has a long name, he/she may have to ask you to change the type size so that the name fits on one line. Show the children how to press the *return* key to create a space under the name.

Organise the children into pairs to take turns at the computer. When there are four or five names on the screen, print out the page and show it to the whole class; then continue.

When everyone has finished, trim the labels to a suitable size and attach them to the children's trays. It is not advisable to let young children do this themselves. If possible, enlist the help of a classroom assistant or parent helper.

Suggestion(s) for extension

Some children may be able to choose the size and colour of the text. Other labels (with more than one word) could be made for different areas of the classroom.

Suggestion(s) for support

If one or two children are relatively confident, appoint them as 'IT monitors': tell the other children that if they need help, they should ask these

children first. Enlist the help of a parent volunteer if possible.

Assessment opportunities
Note the level of independence that individual children demonstrate when carrying out the activity.

Display ideas
A smaller set of name labels could be printed out and used in a display of self-portraits, or used to identify other work on display around the classroom. They could also be used to display the names of children in particular teaching groups.

TOPICAL TITLES

To choose different fonts and text sizes. To centre and colour text. To develop keyboard skills further.
†† *Whole-class discussion; paired activity.*
🕐 *15–30 minutes discussion/demonstration time; 15 minutes computer time.*

Previous skills/knowledge needed
The children should be familiar with a word processing program, and be able to enter and delete text.

Key background information
See notes for 'This is me!' on page 18. This activity builds on previous experience of finding appropriate letter keys and deleting mistakes. It introduces the children to the skills involved in choosing a font type, size and colour. Figure 4 shows some examples of interesting font types (also see photocopiable page 110).

Language to be introduced
Font names and sizes as identified in the program being used, such as *Broadway, Open, Homerton* and *Small/Large Giant*.

Preparation
Make one copy per child of photocopiable page 110. If required, prepare a template page as specified in 'Suggestion(s) for support' below.

Resources needed
One copy per child of photocopiable page 110, a computer with a word processing program, a colour printer, some published books or book covers.

What to do
Show the children some book covers, discussing the information they contain: title, author, illustrator and so on. Suggest that they make a cover for their current topic folder

Figure 4

or book. What should it contain?

Demonstrate how to type in the text for a book cover. Include choosing a font type, size and colour. Invite individual children to have a go while the others watch. Remind the children how to make spaces under words by using the *enter/return* key, and how to delete whole line spaces with the *backspace* key. Encourage them to key in the text first and refine the appearance of the page later. Restrict the number of words to the book's title, the author's name (or authors' names), the class number and the term or year:

> Minibeasts
> by Sheena and Iqbal
> Class 2H
> Autumn 1998

Show the children a copy of photocopiable page 110, and tell them that more copies of it will be near the computer should they need to refer to it.

Suggestion(s) for extension
Some children may wish to include a picture. Give them a

piece of paper of suitable size; when the picture is finished, ask them to leave enough space between two of the lines on their cover to paste in the picture.

Suggestion(s) for support
Selecting fonts and so on is more complicated using some word processing programs than others, and this will affect the amount of support needed. More confident children can be paired with the less confident. If the cover relates to a group topic, several children can work on producing the same cover, providing mutual support.

Some children may need to have the font, size and colour already set up for them. They can enter text onto a prepared template page which has instructions for them to delete:

> [Title]
> [Your name]
> [Class number]

Assessment opportunities
The finished covers may not give a good indication of attainment, as many children will have been supported in some way. The next time a similar activity is undertaken, make sure that all the children work as independently as possible and take a second printout. Look for correct use

INFORMATION TECHNOLOGY

of the *enter/return* key and the *delete* and *backspace* keys. Annotate this with any comments and the date.

Display ideas
The completed topic folders or books, with their printed covers, could be displayed alongside published material on the same subject. They could also be displayed as part of the summative topic display.

Reference to photocopiable sheet
Photocopiable page 110 provides some examples of fonts available in popular word-processing programs, as well as some suggestions for the layout of a book cover.

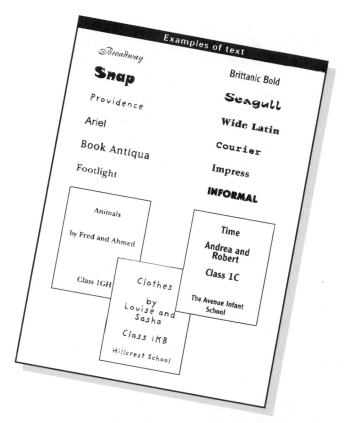

FILLING THE GAPS

To insert and delete text on a computer.
†† *Whole-class discussion; paired activity.*
🕐 *15–20 minutes discussion/demonstration time; 15–20 minutes computer time.*

Previous skills/knowledge needed
The children should be able to enter text and use the *backspace* key for deletion. Their reading ability needs to be in line with the demands of the particular passage of text used in the activity.

Key background information
Cloze procedure is an activity designed to develop children's

skills in reading and comprehension through the use of prediction. A passage of text is produced with certain words missing (often every seventh word). The children have to find the most appropriate word to fill the space. There is not necessarily a 'correct' answer each time, as several words may be acceptable as an answer. The children should use the meaning of the passage and the syntactical clues (sentence structure and grammar) to predict the missing text.

Preparation
Choose passages from current reading books, information books related to a current topic or the current class story. Enter them onto pages in a word-processing package and delete every seventh word. Mark each place where a word has been deleted with an asterisk. If you have access to a scanner that recognises text, this will greatly speed up the process of transferring the passages to the computer.

Resources needed
A computer with a word-processing program, a colour printer, cloze passages saved in the computer or on a floppy disk, a book with a familiar story.

What to do
Read a familiar story to the children, missing out some words and encouraging them to suggest what the words might be. Start with very obvious examples and progress

INFORMATION TECHNOLOGY

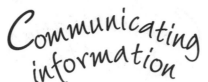

Children whose IT skills are less well-developed may need the support of another child or adult.

Assessment opportunities

Ask the children to time themselves in completing each cloze task, and to write the time taken on a printout of the completed text.

Note the children's capabilities when using the computer. In particular, note how ready they are to enter initial suggestions rather than waiting until they have the 'right' answer; this reflects their confidence in their own ability to edit text on screen.

WHAT'S ON THE MENU?

To become more familiar with the centreing facility of a word processor. To use IT for a purpose in a realistic context.

†† *Whole-class discussion; paired activity.*

🕐 *10–15 minutes discussion/demonstration time; 20–30 minutes computer time.*

---

to those which suggest several possible solutions. Ask the children how they are predicting the words, and encourage appropriate strategies rather than simple guessing.

Demonstrate how similar passages can be completed on the computer screen. Assign appropriate passages (see 'Preparation') for the variety of reading levels in the class, and set up a rota for the children to work in pairs of similar ability. Encourage discussion, and emphasise that there may be several possible alternative words for each gap. Encourage the children to insert several possible solutions and then use the *highlight* and *delete* facilities to make a final choice.

Suggestion(s) for extension

Children could choose passages or write their own, key them in and then 'hide' words by deleting, say, every seventh one. Working in pairs, they could take turns to set and solve the puzzles.

Children could be given the challenge of finding as many appropriate words as possible to fill each space.

Suggestion(s) for support

Lower-attaining children could be given very obvious cloze passages to start with, followed by more challenging ones. The number of letters in the more obvious missing words could be indicated by the number of dashes or asterisks in the space.

Previous skills/knowledge needed

The children should be familiar with a word-processing program and be able to enter, delete and centre text, and to choose the type, size and colour of a font. (See 'Topical titles' on page 19.)

Key background information

See notes for 'This is me!' on page 18. This activity builds on previous experience of handling text. It reinforces centreing and creating spaces with the *enter/return* key. It

could be undertaken when children are involved in food technology activities, or are preparing for a special occasion such as Christmas or a school anniversary.

Preparation
Practise adjusting text to print onto a background. Make copies (as required) of photocopiable pages 111 and 112.

Resources needed
A computer with a word processing program, a colour printer, sample menus (especially ones with centred text), prepared A4 sample menus (photocopiable page 111) and menu backgrounds (photocopiable page 112), writing materials, dictionaries.

What to do
Discuss their favourite foods with the children. Ask them to describe meals they have eaten in restaurants, and focus on the menus and the information they contain. How are the various courses identified – starter, main course, sweet and so on? What would be their 'perfect' meal?

Show them some examples of printed menus, drawing attention to the various fonts used and the way the different courses or types of dish are separated with headings. Draw attention to the use of centreing in most menus.

Remind the children how to select a font and how to resize, colour and centre text. Set them the task of devising their own menus and producing attractive versions on the computer. Organise them into pairs, ensuring (if possible) that any lower-attaining children have the support of a more confident partner. Ask the children to write down their menus on the incomplete menu sheet (photocopiable page 111), checking their spellings with a dictionary, before using the computer.

Before the children print out a final version, give them a background sheet (photocopiable page 112) for their menu. They should print the menu directly onto this background, resizing and centreing it appropriately to fit. Help them to adjust the text margins as necessary. Provide additional copies of the background sheet if these are needed, but encourage the children not to waste copies.

Suggestion(s) for extension
The same techniques could be used in a different context to produce notices for the classroom, such as group lists or monitor rotas, to develop the children's ability to relate the use of centreing to other layout skills.

Suggestion(s) for support
This activity may require the continuous support of an adult, particularly in discussing the final appearance of the menu before printing it out. Most children are likely to need help with printing out, including making sure that the background

selected is the right way up in the printer.

Assessment opportunities
Note the children's level of independence in centreing text and formatting the completed menus. Look out for evidence of higher-attaining children using their existing IT skills in a new context – for example, in producing notices using the skills developed when compiling menus (see 'Suggestion(s) for extension' above).

Display ideas
If there is a 'café' set up in the classroom, the finished menus can be used during role-play.

Reference to photocopiable sheets
The incomplete sample menu on photocopiable page 111 provides some basic ideas to help children think about the content and layout of a menu. They can write their menus on this sheet before keying the text into the computer. Photocopiable page 112 provides a background onto which the completed menus can be printed.

CHEF'S SPECIAL

To position words and numbers on a computer screen using the tab facility.

†† *Whole-class discussion; paired activity.*

🕐 *20–30 minutes discussion/demonstration time; 20–30 minutes computer time.*

Previous skills/knowledge needed

The children should be familiar with a word-processing program and be able to enter, delete and centre text, and to choose the type, size and colour of a font.

Key background information

See 'This is me!' on page 18. This activity builds on previous experience of using a word processor to handle text. It reinforces centreing and creating spaces with the *enter/return* key, and introduces the *tab* key. Setting the context for this activity is important: it should be undertaken only when children are involved in food technology activities.

Language to be introduced

Tab. Vocabulary associated with recipes, such as *ingredients, amount, grams*.

Preparation

Make copies (one of each per child) of photocopiable page

113. Prepare a recipe on screen which is just a paragraph of continuous text, without any formatting. Save this for use by those children who need support with entering text.

Resources needed

A computer with a word processing program, a colour printer, sample menus (preferably ones with the ingredients printed in regular columns), photocopiable page 113.

What to do

Discuss cooking with the children. *What have they observed about how their parents or carers cook? How do adults know what to do and what to use?* Ask them about their own cooking experiences in school. *How did they know what ingredients to use? Where did the teacher get the information?* Share some of your own favourite recipes, emphasising the importance of using the correct amounts in the correct sequence.

Introduce the task of writing a recipe for something they have cooked in school, and printing it for other children to use. Demonstrate how to choose the style, colour and size of font for the recipe (including the use of more than one type size within a recipe). Show how the *tab* key can be used to align text in columns by keying in some ingredients and amounts, for example:

flour	25g
milk	¼ pint
raisins	1 tablespoon

Now ask the children to create a recipe card. Organise them into pairs, making sure (if possible) that any lower-attaining children have the support of a more confident partner. Establish a rota for shared and efficient use of the computer. Give out copies of photocopiable page 113, children can then use this as a background on which to display their printed recipe.

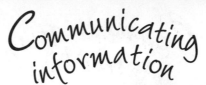

Suggestion(s) for extension
The same techniques could be used in a different context to produce a notice recording scores in PE, or any list with more than one column.

Suggestion(s) for support
This activity may require the continuous support of an adult, particularly in discussing the final appearance of the recipe before printing it out. Most children are likely to need help with printing out, including making sure that the background is the right way up in the printer. If appropriate, children could be given the passage of unformatted text already entered on the screen (see 'Preparation') and asked to arrange it in the form of a conventional recipe.

Assessment opportunities
Note whether children use the *tab* key correctly. Look for evidence of the higher-attaining children using the *tab* key in a new context – for example, in producing tables of PE scores ordered in columns.

Display ideas
If there is a 'café' set up in the classroom, the finished recipes can be used during role-play. They could also be compiled into a class recipe book.

Reference to photocopiable sheet
Photocopiable page 113 provides a background within which the children's completed recipes can be printed.

PEN PORTRAITS

To develop greater familiarity with a touch-sensitive keyboard. To reinforce the skills of using the* enter/return *and* delete *keys.

†† *Whole-class discussion; paired activity.*

🕐 *30 minutes discussion/demonstration time; 20 minutes computer time.*

Previous skills/knowledge needed
The children need to have been introduced to the concept keyboard and to know that pressing it produces text on the computer screen. They should have had some experience in entering text into a word processor.

Key background information
See 'Winter words' on page 14 and 'Ice breaker' on page 16. This activity involves the children in producing the text which will appear when the concept keyboard is pressed. It is split into three stages:

1. The children use a word processor to write information about themselves.

2. The teacher uses this writing, together with photographs of the children, to make an overlay.

3. The children use the overlay to find out facts about each other.

In this activity, the completed overlay is used as a reference tool rather than an aid to writing. More sophisticated versions of this system can be found in public places. For example, a screen in a tourist information centre may have pictures of local attractions which, when pressed, produce maps, details of admission prices and so on.

00	01	02	03	04	05	06	07	08	09	10	11	12	13	14	15
0 0	1	2	3	4	5	6	7	8	9	A	B	C	D	E	F
16	17	18	19	20	21	22	23	24	25	26	27	28	29	30	31
1															
32	33	34	35	36	37	38	39	40	41	42	43	44	45	46	47
2															
48	49	50	51	52	53	54	55	56	57	58	59	60	61	62	63
3															
64	65	66	67	68	69	70	71	72	73	74	75	76	77	78	79
4															
80	81	82	83	84	85	86	87	88	89	90	91	92	93	94	95
5															
96	97	98	99	100	101	102	103	104	105	106	107	108	109	110	111
6															
112	113	114	115	116	117	118	119	120	121	122	123	124	125	126	127
7															

Figure 5a

Language to be introduced
Information.

Preparation
Make sure you are familiar with the system to be used beforehand.

Take individual 'head and shoulders' photographs of the children; or take a class photograph, making sure that each child's face is clearly visible. Use these photographs to produce an overlay sheet. Figure 5a shows a suitable A3 overlay grid. If you are using individual photographs, these will need to be printed at passport size; 32 passport photographs will fit onto an A3 overlay sheet (see Figure 5b). If larger prints are used, two overlays will probably be needed. If you are using a group photograph, print it as large as possible so that the faces are above separate cells of the overlay (see Figure 5c).

Once the overlay is complete, you need to link the cells to the children's names so that when each photograph (or face in a group photograph) is pressed, the correct name appears on the screen. The exact method for this will depend on the particular system being used, but the process is quite straightforward. As well as the name, personal details (see 'What to do') can be linked to the photograph or face by editing the file.

Resources needed
A computer with a word processing program, a touch-sensitive keyboard linked to the computer, an overlay with an associated file, photographs of individual children (or a class photograph), writing materials.

What to do
In the context of work on 'Ourselves' or personal and social education, introduce the idea of 'pen portraits'. Ask the children to suggest what personal details they might include when writing about themselves. In addition to facts such as their age and date of birth, do they think information about their favourite food, sports player or pop group would be appropriate?

Remind them of their previous work with a word processor, including how to use the *enter/return* key to start a new line and the *delete* key to correct mistakes. Set them the task of writing a factfile about themselves. Organise a rota for them to use the computer in pairs, emphasising the support they should give each other as proof-readers. Time at the computer can be saved by asking the children to jot down notes on paper before taking their turn to use the screen.

Once everyone has completed the task, enter their text into the overlay file you have prepared.

Figure 5b

The exact method for this will depend on the system being used. Now set up the computer and concept keyboard and gather the children around it. Invite children to press their own photographs and to read their pen portraits.

Provide opportunities for them to use the overlay individually during the next few days.

Suggestion(s) for extension
More confident children could be encouraged to use the overlay to find out information about other children in the class or their group, which could then be printed out to make a booklet.

Suggestion(s) for support
Children with less secure literacy skills could be provided with a pro-forma to use as a structure for their writing, with headings such as **name**, **birthday** and so on.

Assessment opportunities
Look for children using the *enter/return* and *delete* keys, and note their level of accuracy and confidence. Note how quickly they can find the appropriate letter keys as they enter text on the screen.

Display ideas
When all the information has been entered into the overlay

Figure 5c

file, set up the word processor-concept keyboard link so that it is available in the classroom, corridor or entrance hall, and add a suitable label or sign such as 'Come and find out about Class 3'.

DEAR SIR

To develop word-processing skills related to letter writing, using a conventional layout. To use the justify facility for right and left alignment.

†† *Whole-class discussion; paired activity.*

🕐 *20–30 minutes discussion/demonstration time; 30 minutes computer time.*

Previous skills/knowledge needed
The children should be familiar with a word processing program and be able to enter and delete text.

Key background information
This activity builds on previous experience of finding appropriate letter keys and deleting mistakes. It introduces the *right justify* facility, and allows children to use it in a realistic context.

Language to be introduced
Justify, right justify, left justify.

Preparation
Collect some examples of printed and handwritten letters which follow the conventional layout, particularly the sender's address being placed in the top right-hand corner. Prepare a screen template as shown in 'Suggestion(s) for

support' below. Make one copy per child of photocopiable page 114.

Resources needed
A computer with a word processing program, a printer, examples of printed and handwritten letters (see 'Preparation'), photocopiable page 114, envelopes and stamps for the children's letters.

What to do
Discuss letter writing with the children. Why do people often write letters instead of using a telephone? Show them some examples of letters, pointing out the conventions: the sender's address in the top right-hand corner, the date, 'Dear ...', 'Yours sincerely' and so on.

Demonstrate how to write an address on the computer, and how to right-justify it. Show how to return the subsequent text to left justification. Talk the children through a letter as you write it on the screen. Make a point of jotting down key words (on the screen) when you are thinking about what you want to include in the letter. Use these key words to make sentences and build up the content of the letter. Choose an appropriate concluding sentence and add 'Yours sincerely' or 'With love from' as appropriate.

INFORMATION TECHNOLOGY

```
                                              [address here]
                                              [date]

Dear [                    ]



Yours sincerely,
[your name]
```

Figure 6

Assessment opportunities

Note which children achieve a correct layout, and how successfully the children can shift from one mode of justification to another. Look for evidence of the higher-attaining children using right, left and centre justification in new contexts.

Display ideas

Any replies to the children's letters could be displayed alongside copies of the original letters. A classroom 'Post Office' could be set up, where letters for delivery within the school are 'posted' in a post box.

Reference to photocopiable sheet

Photocopiable page 114 provides some ideas and prompts to get children started with writing letters.

Ask the children to think about someone they would like to write a letter to. It could be a 'thank you' letter to a classroom helper, a 'get well' message to an absent friend or teacher, a letter asking the headteacher to change some aspect of the school's routine, and so on.

Tell the children that they are going to write a letter straight onto the computer screen. They should write in key words as they are thinking of the content. Suggest that the letter contain a minimum of three ideas. If they have difficulty in getting started, refer them to photocopiable page114, which provides some useful prompts. Emphasise that these letters will be sent: they are not pretending to write a letter.

When the letters are finished, provide envelopes and stamps and ask the children to post their letters under the supervision of a parent or carer.

Suggestion(s) for extension

The children could use the same techniques independently to write word-processed letters to other people of their choice.

Suggestion(s) for support

For children who are finding the formatting of a letter difficult, a template could be set up on the screen with appropriate instructions (see Figure 6).

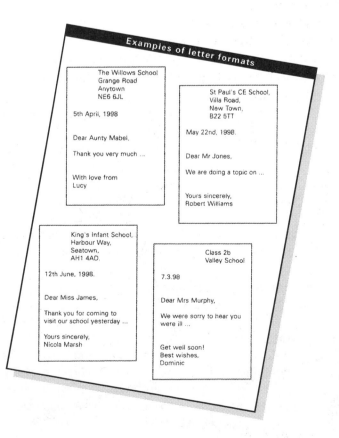

Examples of letter formats

```
The Willows School
Grange Road
Anytown
NE6 6JL

5th April, 1998


Dear Aunty Mabel,

Thank you very much ...


With love from
Lucy
```

```
St Paul's CE School,
Villa Road,
New Town,
B22 5TT

May 22nd, 1998.


Dear Mr Jones,

We are doing a topic on ...


Yours sincerely,
Robert Williams
```

```
King's Infant School,
Harbour Way,
Seatown,
AH1 4AD.

12th June, 1998.


Dear Miss James,

Thank you for coming to
visit our school yesterday ...


Yours sincerely,
Nicola Marsh
```

```
                   Class 2b
                   Valley School

7.3.98


Dear Mrs Murphy,

We were sorry to hear you
were ill ...


Get well soon!
Best wishes,
Dominic
```

HOW IT LOOKS

To insert a picture into a page of text.

♉♉ *Whole-class discussion; paired activity.*

🕐 *20–30 minutes discussion/demonstration time; 15–20 minutes computer time.*

Previous skills/knowledge needed

The children should be competent in generic word-processing skills, as developed in the previous eight activities.

Key background information

This activity depends on the availability of suitable pictures. There are numerous collections of pictures available on disk. These images are known as 'clip art'. Alternatively, pictures made by children using graphics programs can be stored in the same way. Pictures take up a lot of computer memory, so it is a good idea to test whether the system being used will cope with a mixture of text and pictures on the screen. Most modern systems should be capable of this. The more sophisticated the program and computer system being used are, the easier the activity will be.

This activity is best carried out following an educational visit (for example, to a safari park or a public landmark).

Language to be introduced

Clip art, graphics.

Preparation

Prepare a directory containing a suitable number and range of images; this could include scanned versions of the children's drawings. Make sure that these can easily be located on the hard disk or on clearly-labelled floppy disks. Make one copy per child of photocopiable sheet 115.

Resources needed

A computer with a word processing program, appropriate pictures created using a graphics program or scanned versions of the children's drawings, a colour printer, photocopiable page 115.

What to do

Following an educational visit, suggest that the children record what they found out, or their impressions, using brief phrases and drawings. Demonstrate how to place a picture into a page of text on the screen. (The exact method will depend on the particular system being used.) Show the children how to move the picture around the page by dragging, and how to resize a picture using the 'handles' on the frame. Enter some text on the screen and demonstrate how the text can be moved around the picture or vice versa.

Ask each pair of children to create a page for a book about the visit. Restrict the number of ideas contributed by each pair, asking them to choose the most important ones for inclusion on their page. Restrict each pair to one image each, in order to avoid computer memory problems and to save time when printing out. Show them the sample page layouts on photocopiable page 115.

When the children have finished their pages, ask them to save their work so that you can print it out later.

Suggestion(s) for extension

In order to consolidate the skills involved in mixing text and graphics, some children may be able to use the same techniques when recording other work, for example in history or geography.

Suggestion(s) for support

The difficulty of this activity will depend on the program

INFORMATION TECHNOLOGY

classroom or library. Printouts of some pages could be displayed individually, alongside the children's comments on the techniques involved.

Reference to photocopiable sheet
Photocopiable page 115 shows some examples of different layouts of text and pictures.

SHORT AND SWEET

To practise drafting and redrafting text using a word processor.

†† *Whole-class discussion; activity in groups of 3 or 4.*

🕐 *20–30 minutes discussion/demonstration time; 30–45 minutes computer time.*

Previous skills/knowledge needed
The children should be familiar with a word processing program and be able to enter and delete text.

Key background information
Since the amount of time that each child can spend at the computer is usually limited, many activities require some kind of preparation beforehand. However, a major advantage of using a word processor is that you can 'brainstorm' ideas on the screen and then add and delete them as you work. Children should be encouraged to use the screen as a notebook; but this obviously takes up more screen time. Organising children into small groups for computer work is a good way to optimise the time spent. Three is an ideal number, four a maximum.

This activity builds on previous experience of finding the appropriate letter keys and deleting mistakes. It alllows children to use IT in a realistic context. The piece of writing involved is kept short to allow optimum use of computer time.

and computer system being used. It may be necessary to provide adult support. A group of two or three children can be taken carefully through each step to ensure that they make progress and are not discouraged by making too many mistakes.

Assessment opportunities
Those children who can carry out this task independently will be working at (or beyond) Level 3 in this strand of IT. Try to observe them while they are working at the computer to ascertain their level of independence and technical skill.

Display ideas
The completed book about the visit can be displayed in the

INFORMATION TECHNOLOGY

Language to be introduced

The terms *draft*, *redraft* and *edit* should be used when discussing the activity.

Preparation

Find a selection of appropriate short poems and very short (one-page) stories. Useful sources of short poems include *Skip Across the Ocean* edited by Floella Benjamin, illustrated by Sheila Moxley (Frances Lincoln, 1995) and *The Grasshopper Laughs* edited by Michael Bird, illustrated by Andrew Stooke (Faber, 1995).

Resources needed

A computer with a word processing program, a printer, a selection of short poems, a selection of very short stories.

What to do

Read a selection of short poems and mini-stories to the children. Point out the ways in which the authors convey meaning using only a few words. Ask the children to suggest short phrases which use the minimum of words to describe an event, a place or a person.

Gather the children around the computer screen (this may need to be done a group at a time) and act as scribe while they suggest concise ideas for a poem or story. If necessary, suggest a theme. Enter all their suggestions, then talk them through a process of selection. *What shall we keep? What shall we reject for the moment?* Aim to

complete a four- or six-line poem or story. Avoid rhyming couplets, and encourage the children to experiment with repetition.

Organise the children into groups of three or four, and arrange a rota to use the computer. Ask them to think about a topic for their poem or story before it is their turn. When they come to use the computer, they will have to work together quickly to complete a six-line poem or story. Each group should be allowed 30 minutes for the first session; if necessary, they will have to save their unfinished work and return to it later.

Suggestion(s) for extension

Some children might enjoy writing a familiar verse on the screen and then deleting all but the most significant words. *Is the meaning still apparent? What is lost when some words are removed? Is it still a poem?*

Suggestion(s) for support

Careful grouping should ensure that lower-attaining children have support. The introductory screen work could be repeated by a teaching assistant or volunteer. It should be emphasised that all suggestions are worthwhile.

Assessment opportunities

Look for evidence of children using this technique in other contexts. This would indicate a high level of IT skill. The technical competence required to enter text is only a means to the ultimate objective of enabling children to harness these skills appropriately in the course of their everyday work.

Display ideas

The finished pieces of writing could be printed out and bound together to make a class book entitled *The Book of Small Poems* or *Thirty Tiny Tales*.

THE WORDS THAT COUNT

To understand the potential of the word processor as a tool for creative writing.

†† Whole-class discussion; activity in pairs or groups of 3.

🕐 15–30 minutes discussion/demonstration time; 45 minutes computer time.

Previous skills/knowledge needed

The children should be familiar with a word processing

program. They should be able to enter, delete and justify text and to select the type, size and colour of a font.

Key background information

See 'Short and sweet' on page 31. This activity combines the use of the word processor to 'brainstorm' ideas with some preparation away from the screen.

Preparation

Prepare a word bank relating to a current topic, theme or class story. If appropriate, prepare a sheet similar to Figure 7 for each pair or group of children.

Resources needed

A computer with a word processing program, a printer, a word bank sheet (if required), writing materials.

What to do

Tell the children that you have chosen some words relating to the current topic, theme or class story. Display these on the board. Ask the children whether they can think of some more. Now organise them into pairs or threes. Tell them that they are going to enter their own words (as well as the

Figure 7 – Word banks

THE SEA

SPRING

HAPPINESS IS...

a new baby

playing with friends

chocolate ice-cream

a pet kitten

INFORMATION
TECHNOLOGY

ones you have provided) on the screen and use them as prompt words or building blocks to construct a poem. Each pair or group can brainstorm words and ideas on a copy of the prepared sheet (see 'Preparation') while waiting to use the computer. They should make the finished piece as attractive as possible, using an appropriate font type, size and colour.

Suggestion(s) for extension
More confident children can be given a free choice of topic and asked to choose all the prompt words. This will develop their experience of using the computer for creative work. They could use a thesaurus to find synonyms.

Suggestion(s) for support
Careful grouping can provide less confident children with support. Some prompt words from your word bank could be entered on the screen before the children start working. The prepared sheet could be augmented by adding more words for some children.

Assessment opportunities
Look for evidence of children using the computer as a notebook in other contexts. This would indicate a high level of IT skill. The necessary confidence should be encouraged.

Display ideas
The finished poems could be displayed or bound into a book and put in the poetry section of the library.

WHO'S WHO

To develop familiarity with the uses of a touch-sensitive keyboard. To practise the keyboard skills of entering text using the enter/return and delete keys.

†† *Whole-class discussion; activity in groups of 3.*

🕓 *30 minutes discussion/demonstration time; 20 minutes computer time; another session for interviews.*

Previous skills/knowledge needed
The children need to have been introduced to the concept

keyboard and to know that pressing it produces text on the computer screen. They should have had some experience of entering text into a word processor.

Key background information
See 'Pen portraits' on page 25. This activity requires the children to produce the text which will appear when the concept keyboard is pressed. It is divided into four stages:
1. Collecting information.
2. Entering the information onto a computer screen.
3. Combining the text with photographs to make an overlay.
4. Using the overlay to find out information.

Here, as in the 'Pen portraits' activity, the completed overlay is used as a reference tool rather than an aid to writing.

Preparation
Make sure you are familiar with the system beforehand.

Take individual photographs of each member of staff, and use these to produce an overlay sheet. For each photograph, link the relevant cells to the staff member's name (see 'Pen portraits' on page 25). The exact method will depend on the system being used.

Inform your colleagues of the activity and the kind of questions the children are likely to ask. Find out when an interview would be most convenient for them.

Make one copy per child of photocopiable page 116 (if required).

Resources needed
A computer with a word processing program, a touch-sensitive keyboard linked to the computer, an overlay with an associated file, photographs of individual members of staff (or a school photograph), writing materials, photocopiable sheet 116 (if required).

What to do
In the context of work on topics such as *Our school* or *People who help us*, introduce the idea of collecting information about members of staff. Another appropriate context would be the preparation for a parents' evening or open day. In discussing how the information could be collected and presented, see whether the children suggest

INFORMATION
TECHNOLOGY

(using the word processor) to guide people on how to find the information; the children could use their ability to select fonts and centre text in this new context.

Suggestion(s) for support
Children with less secure language skills could be provided with a pro-forma (photocopiable page 116) to provide a structure for their interviews. Careful grouping should ensure that they have peer support. Colleagues could be made aware beforehand of those children who are likely to need help during the interviews.

Assessment opportunities
Look for evidence of children using the *enter/return* and *delete* keys, and note their level of accuracy and confidence. Note how quickly they can find the appropriate letter keys as they enter text on the screen.

Display ideas
When all the information has been entered, set up the word processor-concept keyboard link so that it is available in the classroom, corridor or entrance hall. Add a suitable label or sign, such as *Who's who at the Grange Primary School*.

Reference to photocopiable sheet
Photocopiable page 116 is a pro-forma 'Teacher profile' sheet which could be used by the children in conducting their interviews (see 'Suggestion(s) for support').

the method used in 'Pen portraits'; if not, direct the discussion towards this.

Discuss the kind of information that would be appropriate. For example, if parents are going to use this system when they come for a consultation meeting, perhaps the information should include directions to each teacher's classroom. Come to a general agreement about what questions should be asked of each member of staff, and ask the children to jot these down. Alternatively, photocopiable page 116 could be provided as a pro-forma.

Divide the children into groups of three and assign each group to collect information about one member of staff. Depending on the number of staff, the working groups may need to be smaller or larger. Set up times for interviews according to what has been agreed with your colleagues.

When the children have carried out their interviews, set up a rota for them to enter the information they have gathered into a word processor. Remind them of their previous work, including how to use the *enter/return* key to start a new line and the *delete* key to correct mistakes. Emphasise that they should take turns to enter text, and that they should act as proof-readers for each other.

Once everyone has completed the task, enter the text into the overlay file you have prepared. Then set up the computer with the concept keyboard and gather the children around it. Invite individual children to press the photographs and read the information. Discuss how this system might be used by new pupils and their parents, by a new member of staff, or by visitors to the school. Provide opportunities for the children to use the overlay individually during the next few days.

Suggestion(s) for extension
More confident children could be asked to make a notice

Teacher profile

Name _____ Class _____

How long have you been a teacher?

How long have you taught at this school?

What do you like about teaching here?

Do you have a favourite subject?

Which age group do you like teaching best?

Would you like to be a headteacher?

Why, or why not?

What do you like doing in your spare time?

WAX LYRICAL

To further understand the potential of the word processor as a tool for creative writing. To practise 'copy and paste'.

†† *Whole-class discussion; individuals, pairs or groups of 3 for activity.*

🕐 *15–30 minutes discussion/demonstration time; 45 minutes computer time.*

Previous skills/knowledge needed

The children should be familiar with a word processing program. They should be able to enter, justify and delete text, and to select the type, size and colour of a font. They should have some experience of composition in music.

Key background information

See 'The words that count' on page 33. This activity should be undertaken following work on composition in music, creating tunes – as in the activities 'If you're happy and you

know it' (page 58) and 'From Major to Minor' (page 60) – or simple rhythm patterns.

Language to be introduced

Lyrics, cut, paste, copy.

Preparation

If appropriate, obtain a cassette recorder and some taped songs which combine music and lyrics.

Resources needed

A computer with a word processing program, a printer, a cassette recorder and taped songs (if appropriate).

What to do

Discuss the methods that professional songwriters adopt when they are composing. Some start with the words, some with the tune; some try to write both at the same time. Tell them about famous songwriters who have worked in partnership, such as Gilbert and Sullivan or Lennon and McCartney. The children may be familiar with compositions such as 'Yellow Submarine'. If appropriate, play extracts from some songs, drawing attention to the relationship between the music and the lyrics.

Remind the children of the tunes or rhythm patterns they have previously composed, and suggest that they think about the mood created by the music. Ask the children to think about suitable words to go with their tunes/rhythms, introducing the word *lyrics*.

Briefly recap on how to enter text, and show them how you might start entering ideas directly onto the screen: 'Yes, I think the music sounds like a party, so I'll type in *noise, cakes, friends, games...*'. Draw attention to the fact that in songs, the words usually rhyme. Ask them to suggest words that rhyme with the ones on the screen. Key in suitable rhyming words on the screen, rejecting those which don't have any possible connection with the theme. Now insert the rhyming words in appropriate places, talking through how you move the cursor and enter the new text. '*Noise?* Yes, *boys, toys... Cakes?* Yes, *bakes... Friends?* Yes, *sends... Games?* Yes, *names...*'

Discuss the use of repetition in song lyrics, and show the children how to copy by highlighting the required text and clicking on the *copy* icon. Demonstrate how this can be pasted as many times as you wish by moving the cursor to the required position and clicking on the *paste* icon.

Set the task, which is for the children to write lyrics for their original tunes/rhythms and to print them out. Organise the grouping according to how the original tunes were composed – by individuals, pairs or threes – and set up a rota for using the computer.

Suggestion(s) for extension

More confident children could be asked to think of

INFORMATION
TECHNOLOGY

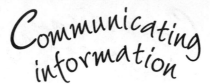

imaginative ways of presenting the lyrics. If they have previously used clip art, they could insert appropriate pictures.

Suggestion(s) for support

Some children are likely to need help in thinking of appropriate vocabulary. Once they have identified a theme for their lyrics, provide some suggestions to get them started. They might also need help to avoid producing doggerel. Try to provide adult support to review their efforts before finally printing them out.

Assessment opportunities

Note which children use the copy and paste technique successfully. Look for children who understand that the copied text remains available until a different section is copied (and thus don't re-copy unnecessarily).

Performance ideas

Children could perform their songs for the rest of the class or in assembly. Compositions involving only percussion could be performed 'live'; but those composed on the computer will need to be sung with the music as a backing track.

NEWS DESK

To develop confidence in word-processing skills and desktop publishing skills. To use IT for a real purpose: producing a newsletter or newspaper for actual readers.

†† *Whole-class together for discussion, working in groups of 3 or 4 for activity.*

🕒 *Extended computer time and time away from the computer over a period of a few days.*

Previous skills/knowledge needed

This activity calls on a number of skills related to 'desktop publishing': word processing; creating a layout; incorporating pictures into pages of text; copying and inserting text and pictures. The IT skills required should not be beyond the capabilities of Year 2 children, provided they are given an appropriate degree of support.

Key background information

IT is classified as a core learning skill, alongside literacy and numeracy. In the same way that reading and number skills are taught so that they can be used, IT skills should be taught in relation to a real context. The aim of this activity is to encourage the children to see the use of IT as a means to an end, not an end in itself. The computer is used as a convenient tool for production. It is quite appropriate to integrate some of the 'old' technology into the activity, such as literally 'cutting and pasting' sheets of paper and writing in notebooks.

Language to be introduced

Vocabulary associated with newspapers can be used: *story, piece, feature, news item, headline, sub-heading, deadline, editor, sub-editor, reporter.*

Preparation

One of the most important aspects of this activity is the speed at which the newsletter will be produced. Time should be set aside so that the usual timetable can be abandoned for an extended period: several mornings, afternoons or days. Make several copies of photocopiable page 117 and cut out the labels.

Resources needed

As many computers as possible (a reciprocal arrangement can often be made with colleagues), examples of real newspapers (especially those targeted at children), a camera (with access to quick processing of film), a word processing program (if possible, one which can format pages into two columns), notebooks, writing materials, photocopiable page 117.

The support of an adult confident in IT will be very useful.

Indeed, it is advisable not to carry out this activity without some extra help in the classroom. Given enough notice, LEA advisors can often be persuaded to take part.

What to do

Establish the context by suggesting that the children make a newsletter or newspaper for another school or their parents (or possibly as a supplement to a local paper). Show the children examples of such publications and discuss their common characteristics: headlines and sub-headings; a balance of text, pictures and white space. Discuss the content and the kind of language used.

Organise the whole class into groups to produce a newsletter or paper. Small groups can be assigned specific roles such as the sports desk, news desk, community information, art department, photographers and so on. Try to create a spirit of urgency in order to maintain the pace: news is only news for a very short time!

The process of making a newspaper or newsletter is likely to include:

▲ interviews with teachers, other members of staff, the lollipop person, the community police officer and so on;

▲ surveys of children in other classes to find out their favourite football teams, pop groups and so on;

▲ first-hand investigative reports – for example, about school meals or playground litter;

▲ factual research from books;

▲ individual accounts of experiences, such as 'My Ballet Lessons' or 'My Trip to EuroDisney'.

Reporters' notebooks could be provided, and the children's notes entered into a word processor and refined into news reports or articles. Adults could act as 'secretaries' to speed up the process and provide support where needed.

If you have access to a digital camera, the children can take photographs to illustrate their writing and insert these directly into the text on screen. If they are using a conventional camera, photographs can be scanned in (perhaps using equipment at a neighbouring school or teachers' centre). Alternatively, spaces can be left in the text and photographs stuck onto the page before it is photocopied.

The children will be involved in choosing appropriate font types and sizes, justifying text and deciding on the layout of each article and page. They will need a good deal of adult support. Unless you have the assistance of local newspaper staff, it will probably be most effective to keep the page size to A4 and produce a more manageable 'magazine' publication, rather than attempting to follow the complex format of a tabloid or broadsheet newspaper.

INFORMATION
TECHNOLOGY

Suggestion(s) for extension and support

Careful allocation of tasks and different levels of teacher/ adult support should ensure that all the children in the class work at a level appropriate to their ability and confidence. Group work should allow individual creativity and peer support to be integrated into the whole project.

Assessment opportunities

Do not attempt to assess specific IT skills closely during this activity: most of your time will be taken up with keeping the whole project going. However, try to keep first- and second-draft material to refer to later in order to ascertain individuals' progression through the project.

Display ideas

Having a real context is essential to this activity. Try to organize for copies of the newspaper or newsletter to be sold by the local newsagent. Alternatively, sections could be inserted into existing newspapers by arrangement. Many newspapers are keen to develop such community links. Parents are an obvious readership; but the wider and more public the audience is, the more meaningful the activity will be.

Reference to photocopiable sheet

Photocopiable page 117 provides labels for the various departments of a newspaper office. Copies of these labels can be attached to desks, work folders, equipment and so on in the course of the work.

News office signs

EDITOR

NEWS DESK

SPORT

JOKES

ADVERTISING

SALES

TAKE A PENCIL FOR A WALK

To introduce painting with coloured light on the computer screen. To practise mouse control. To introduce the 'fill' facility.

†† *Whole-class discussion; paired activity.*

🕐 *15 minutes demonstration/discussion time; 15 minutes computer time.*

Previous skills/knowledge needed

The children need to be able to move a cursor using a mouse, and to carry out single and double clicks.

Key background information

Representational images are more difficult to create with a mouse than with a pencil or brush. Children who are confident with a paintbrush may be frustrated when trying to paint with a mouse. Therefore the most appropriate introductory activities involve those tasks which the computer can perform best, such as filling large spaces with colour and changing one colour to another.

Language to be introduced

Tool, boundary, edge, fill.

Preparation

Make several copies of photocopiable page 118.

Resources needed

A computer with a paint program, a colour printer (essential), photocopiable page 118.

INFORMATION TECHNOLOGY

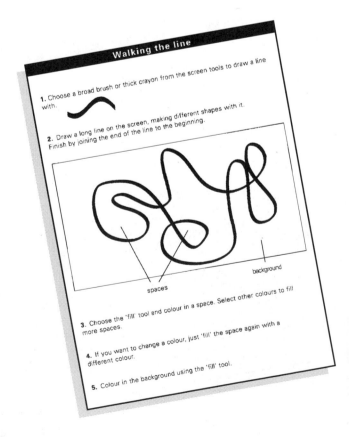

What to do

Demonstrate how to 'walk' the drawing/painting tool on the page by simply moving it around the screen at random, eventually joining the line at the starting point. Don't create too many loops. Ask the children to choose some colours, and show them how to fill the spaces with these colours. Do some colours look better than others?

Remind the children how to click and double click as appropriate (this will depend on the particular program being used) in order to choose colours from the available palette. Organise the children into pairs for computer work. Set the task, which is:

▲ to paint a single line with the painting tool, joining the ends to form a continuous, overlapping loop; and

▲ to fill the spaces created with colour.

Draw the children's attention to photocopiable page 118, which has step-by-step instructions for them to consult if necessary.

Suggestion(s) for extension

Children can be asked to select a variety of shades or tones for a given colour.

Suggestion(s) for support

This activity can be undertaken by all children, no matter what level they are working at; it enables all to achieve a satisfying result. It might be helpful to introduce the activity by asking the children to draw loops on paper and colour them in using paint or crayon. If appropriate, talk through the instructions on photocopiable page 118.

Assessment opportunities

Note how successfully children use the colour options and the *fill* tool. Look for children exploring menus and then returning to the original tools and colours.

Display ideas

The finished colour designs could be displayed around the school, or used as book covers.

Reference to photocopiable sheet

Photocopiable page 118 provides step-by-step instructions for carrying out the activity.

INFORMATION TECHNOLOGY

STAMP IT OUT

To introduce the use of 'stamps'. To refine the skills of 'dragging and dropping'.

†† *Whole-class discussion; paired activity.*

🕐 *20 minutes discussion/demonstration time; 15–20 minutes computer time.*

Previous skills/knowledge needed

The children need to be able to move a cursor using a mouse, and to carry out single and double clicks. Some may already have used the 'drag and drop' technique in another context. If not, this activity provides a useful introduction to it.

Key background information

Representational images are more difficult to create with a mouse than with a pencil or brush. The most appropriate introductory activities thus involve tasks which the computer can do best, such as the use of 'stamps'. These are small pictures which have been created on a computer. They can be placed anywhere on the page; some programs allow them to be resized to a limited extent. They can be used creatively to make patterns or group pictures such as flocks, herds or swarms of animals.

Language to be introduced

Stamp, enlarge, reduce, menu, drag, drop.

Preparation

Check the stamps available on the computer and consider how they might be grouped.

Resources needed

A computer with a paint program which includes a stamp facility, a colour printer (this is essential).

What to do

Demonstrate the stamp facility, pointing out its usefulness in making repeat patterns or scenes with lots of the same image such as flowers, animals, birds or fish. Emphasise (by repeating) how to fix the position of stamps and how to

ORMATION
HNOLOGY

'A flock of sheep'

'An attitude of cats'

the process of selecting, dragging and fixing is more important than the product, so try to create opportunities for yourself or a classroom assistant to note how individual children carry out the activity.

Display ideas
The finished patterns could be used as book covers. The 'group' pictures could be used as part of a display about collective nouns (a *herd* of cows, a *flock* of sheep, and so on).

GET INTO SHAPE

To introduce the autoshape facility. To practise using 'fill'.

†† *Whole-class discussion; paired activity.*

🕐 *20 minutes discussion/demonstration time; 15 minutes computer time.*

Previous skills/knowledge needed
The children need to be able to move a cursor using a mouse and to carry out single or double clicks. They should recognise the 'toolbar' included in a graphics package, and be able to select a tool or facility from it.

Key background information
This activity demonstrates how the computer can be used

delete them. The exact technique will depend on the program being used.

Organise the children into pairs and arrange a rota for computer work. Give them a choice of two activities: either to create a pattern or to create a group picture (such as a swarm of bees, a flock of sheep or a herd of cows). Encourage them to create a suitable background first – perhaps a field and sky, or a lake and shore – using the fill tool. Restrict the number of different stamps they can use in a pattern to two or three.

Suggestion(s) for extension
The more confident children may be able to create their own stamps, say by drawing a flower first and then 'cutting it out' with the appropriate tool. This requires a high degree of skill, and some programs designed for Key Stage 1 do not have this facility (though all of the more sophisticated ones have it).

Suggestion(s) for support
Careful pairing can provide support for less confident children. Some children may need adult help in selecting and manipulating the stamps.

Assessment opportunities
Look for children using the stamp facility in appropriate contexts, rather than simply using it as an easy way to create a picture from scratch. As with many IT activities,

to generate images automatically. The 'autoshape' facility produces ready-made shapes which can be altered in size. For example, a square can be selected and positioned on the page; then, using the dragging technique, the size of the square can be adjusted. Most programs allow the shapes to be open or filled, and the outline (for an open shape) or the whole shape (for a filled shape) to be in colour.

Many paintings by Mondrian are composed largely of regular shapes. Most of the shapes are linked in some way, and the background is therefore divided into irregular shapes.

Language to be introduced
Regular shapes, overlap, background, irregular shapes, Mondrian.

Preparation
Obtain some prints or postcards of Mondrian paintings from art/craft shops or stationers.

Resources needed
An art program which has the 'autoshape' facility; prints or postcards of Mondrian paintings.

What to do
Show the children a selection of Mondrian pictures, inviting their comments. Draw their attention to the simplicity of the concept: arranging shapes together in a pleasing way. *How many shapes are there? Do the spaces also make shapes? Do the colours go together well?*

Demonstrate how to select the autoshape facility and how to place a shape on the page, alter its size and colour. Remind the children how to use the fill option to paint several enclosed areas in the same colour. Try to include some 'deliberate' mistakes so that the children can see how to correct, adjust or make a completely fresh start.

Organise the children into pairs. Introduce the task, which is to emulate Mondrian's paintings on the computer. Restrict the number of shapes in the picture to a maximum of five or six, and suggest that only one or two 'overlaps'

for each shape be used. Emphasise the contribution that the 'spaces' make to the final picture.

Suggestion(s) for extension
Some children may enjoy the challenge of using only one basic colour, but changing the shade or tone so that no two adjacent areas are the same. This is dependent on the program being used having a 'colour mixing' facility which allows the user to 'mix' colours on screen, adjusting the amount of each primary colour to acquire the required shade. Most art programs have this facility. Like many computer facilities, it is difficult to describe but quite straightforward to use!

Suggestion(s) for support
Encourage the children to experiment. Less confident children are often reluctant to make a start for fear of making mistakes. Emphasise the fact that the computer has infinite 'patience'. Minor mistakes can be rectified quickly, or a completely fresh start can be made. You can act as a role model when demonstrating the program.

Assessment opportunities
This activity can be used to assess the extent to which children can: use the mouse to select, drag and drop; use the fill facility; mix colours; save, and print out independently. If they are keeping their own records of achievement (see the comments on pupil records in the Appendix on page 108), these items should be included.

Display ideas
The finished can be used as a wall display, perhaps related to work on shapes. The better quality the colour printer is, the more pleasing the images will be. It may thus be worth saving images and printing them on a higher-quality printer than you have in the classroom. (Of course, this

consideration has to be balanced with the need for the children to see immediate results.)

LOOK, NO SCISSORS!

To introduce and practise 'cut and paste' techniques. To understand and appreciate the power of the computer to generate graphic images.

†† *Whole-class discussion; paired activity.*

🕐 *30–40 minutes discussion/demonstration time; 30 minutes computer time.*

Previous skills/knowledge needed

The children need confidence in using a painting program: choosing brush sizes, colours and so on. They need to have developed competence in using the mouse to draw, select, drag and drop.

Key background information

This activity illustrates the power of the computer relative to traditional methods of creating art. It involves drawing an image on the screen – say a flower or a butterfly – and then 'cutting' it out. The toolbar icon for this is usually a craft knife. A scissors icon usually denotes that only rectangular shapes can be cut out using the tool. The more refined 'craft knife' cutting operation demands quite good control, as the outline of the image on the screen has to be traced over with the pointer.

The first time that children see a shape cut from the page being used as a 'motif' with which to 'stamp' the page, or as a 'pattern pencil' or 'magic brush' (imparting many different colours and motifs to the page), they are usually fascinated. Working with IT can provide many such opportunities for developing an appreciation of the use of technology in art and design.

Language to be introduced

Cut and paste.

Preparation

Obtain some prints, postcards, wallpaper or wrapping paper showing William Morris patterns (or similar repeating designs). These are readily available from stationers, art/craft shops or wallpaper retailers. Make several copies of photocopiable page 119.

Resources needed

An art program with the 'cut and paste' facility; prints, postcards or paper showing William Morris designs; photocopiable sheet 119.

What to do

Demonstrate how the cutting tool works. Paint randomly on the screen, then select the 'cutting' tool and trace round a small area of your picture. Use this to 'stamp' or 'paste' other areas of the screen with the same image. Once the children have seen this process a few times, ask them how they think this facility might be useful. Draw out the fact that it could be used to create repeating patterns.

Next, show the children some examples of William Morris' artwork. Ask them to spot the recurring images. If possible, cut out a piece of the pattern and use it to identify other occurrences of the same image. Is the pattern a regular one? How far is it on the picture before the pattern starts again?

Paint a background on a new page using the 'fill' tool and then draw two different flowers, side by side; cut one out and use it to 'stamp' or 'paste' the same image across the page, leaving spaces for the second flower. Cut out the second flower and fill in the spaces to create a pattern. (Some programs will allow you to use the cut-out image on a completely new page, but with others you will lose the image when opening a new page.)

Organise the children into pairs. Explain the challenge: to design some (A4) wrapping paper for small gifts, using the method you have shown them. Variations could include paper for Christmas, birthday or Mother's Day presents, or wallpaper for a model house. Finally, refer the children to photocopiable page 119,

INFORMATION TECHNOLOGY

which presents step-by-step instructions to the activity should they need them.

Suggestion(s) for extension

The more ambitious the child's design is, the more it will require confidence and sophisticated IT skills to create. Encourage children to experiment with their original images and subsequent patterns. Some may be able to use the 'zoom' facility to refine their designs.

Suggestion(s) for support

Encourage the children to experiment. Minor mistakes can be rectified quickly, or a completely fresh start can be made. You can act as a role model when demonstrating the program, so try to include some 'deliberate' mistakes as you go along.

Assessment opportunities

This activity can be used to assess the extent to which children can: use the mouse successfully to select, drag and drop; use the fill facility; use the cutting/pasting tool accurately; save; and print out independently. If they are keeping their own records of achievement (see the Assessment guide on page 138), these items should be included on the record sheet.

Display ideas

If possible, the finished patterns should be used for a real purpose such as wrapping small presents. The children's work could be displayed alongside William Morris prints and other types of patterned design. It could also be used as wallpaper for a doll's house.

Reference to photocopiable sheet

Photocopiable page 119 provides step-by-step instructions for carrying out the activity.

Wallpaper paste

1. Paint two flower heads. 'Cut' one out using the cutting tool. You can find this tool by selecting it from the toolbar. It might look like this:

2. Stamp the cut-out flower in a pattern on the screen. Leave spaces for the second flower.

3. Cut out the second flower. Use it to fill the spaces on the screen.

COLOUR SWOPS

To further understand and appreciate the power of the computer to generate graphic images. To practise using the 'fill' tool. To practise retrieving a file. To practise printing out independently.

†† *Whole-class discussion; paired activity.*

⏰ *20–30 minutes discussion/demonstration time; 15–20 minutes computer time.*

Previous skills/knowledge needed

The children should be able to move a cursor using a mouse and carry out single and double clicks. They should recognise the 'toolbar' included in a graphics package and be able to select a tool or facility from it. They need to have already produced a picture or pattern, and this needs to have been saved.

Key background information

One of the major advantages of the computer over conventional media is its ability to change colours instantly. This can be achieved using the 'fill' tool: simply choosing a different colour and 'over-painting' the existing one. More sophisticated programs allow all occurrences of a particular colour to be changed at once. For example, all the green trees in a picture could suddenly become red to indicate autumn.

Language to be introduced

Mix, over-paint.

Preparation

Make sure that the children's previously saved pictures or patterns are easily available on the hard disk or a clearly-labelled floppy disk. Prepare a picture of a face or a landscape to use in your demonstration. Provide some 'clip art' images for any children who do not have a picture of their own. (See 'Suggestion(s) for support' below.)

Pictures take up a lot of computer memory, so you will need plenty of space on the hard disk for this activity; a good alternative might be to provide individual floppy disks on which the children can save their own work. (See the Introduction on page 6.)

Resources needed

An art program with the 'fill' option, a colour printer, children's previously created pictures or patterns saved on the computer (or on a floppy disk), a teacher-created picture of a face or a landscape saved on the computer.

What to do

Discuss the frustration caused in painting (by conventional means) when you realise that you have not used quite the right colour. Talk about famous painters and how they would cope with this situation. Do you think they always got it right first time? If not, what did they do?

Load up your own previously saved picture, talking through the process: 'It's in a directory called Miss Jones, and I called it 'face1' so I'd remember it was a face...'. When the picture appears on the screen, remind the children how to use the fill option to paint several enclosed areas in the same colour. Talk about the use of colour and ask the children to suggest alternatives; as they make suggestions, change the colours on screen. Include some 'deliberate' mistakes, so the children can see how to fill again with another colour.

Organise the children into pairs. Introduce the task, which is:

1. To find and open their previously saved picture so it appears on the screen.
2. To experiment with different colour combinations.
3. To print out two differently coloured versions of the picture.

Remind the children to save their alternative version under a different name from the original, so that both versions remain on disk.

Suggestion(s) for extension

Some children may enjoy the challenge of using only one basic colour, changing the shade or tone to ensure that no two adjacent areas are the same (see 'Get into shape' on page 42).

Suggestion(s) for support

If some children have not managed to save a picture beforehand, provide some ready-made examples. These could be taken from collections of clip art; or other children could be asked to share their own pictures. Encourage the less confident

INFORMATION TECHNOLOGY

children to try and experiment with colours.

Assessment opportunities

This activity can be used to assess whether the children can: use the mouse successfully; use the fill facility; mix colours; retrieve and save; and print out independently. If they are keeping their own records of achievement (see the Appendix on page 108), these items should be included.

Display ideas

Two differently-coloured versions of the same picture could be displayed alongside prompts written to generate comments about the effect of each one. Why are certain colour combinations more appealing than others? Does the 'mood' of the picture change when different colours are used? A colour wheel showing primary and secondary colours could be displayed alongside the children's pictures. Samples of wallpaper with the same pattern in different colours could be displayed on a large sheet of backing paper.

Resources needed

An art program with the 'autoshape' option, a colour printer.

What to do

Remind the children about the 'autoshape' facility (or introduce them to it), showing them how to select, move and resize different shapes. The exact technique will depend on the particular program being used.

Use the 'fill' tool to create a dark background as a basis for a 'space' picture. Start to build up a picture of a rocket, drawing on the children's suggestions. Discuss how they could add planets, using the circle shape. Organise the children into pairs and set the task: to create a space picture

PLANET OF THE SHAPES

To develop mouse skills further. To select, resize and rotate shapes using the 'autoshape' facility.

†† *Whole-class discussion; paired activity.*

🕐 *10–15 minutes discussion/demonstration time; 15–20 minutes computer time.*

Previous skills/knowledge needed

The children need to be able to move a cursor using a mouse, and to carry out single or double clicks. They should recognise the 'toolbar' included in a graphics package and be able to select a tool or facility from it.

Key background information

This activity is best undertaken in the context of work on a related subject, such as 'Shape' in mathematics or 'The Earth and beyond' in science. It extends the use of the 'autoshape' facility used in 'Get into shape' on page 42.

Language to be introduced

Autoshape.

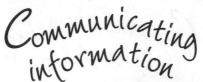

using the autoshapes and any other tools they may be familiar with.

Suggestion(s) for extension

Some children may be able to use reference books to find the relative sizes of the planets, and adjust the sizes of the planets on screen to reflect this information (roughly rather than precisely). The more confident children should be encouraged to print out their work independently.

Suggestion(s) for support

Some children will need the support of an adult or a more confident partner when carrying out the task.

Assessment opportunities

This activity can be used to assess whether the children can: use the mouse successfully; use the fill facility; select the appropriate tool from the toolbar; and select and resize shapes. To draw a rocket using squares, rectangles and triangles requires a high degree of accuracy. Look for those children who have developed the necessary skill in controlling the mouse. If they are keeping their own records of achievement (see page 108), these items should be included.

Display ideas

The finished pictures could be used as covers or title pages for topic books or folders on 'Space', or used as a background for paintings of alien life-forms.

UNDERWATER

To develop mouse skills further. To select, resize and 'paste' shapes. To combine autoshapes with freehand work, judging which is more appropriate. To load a program, save and print out with increasing independence.

†† *Whole-class discussion; paired activity.*

🕐 *20 minutes discussion/demonstration time; 20–30 minutes computer time.*

Previous skills/knowledge needed

The children should be familiar with the painting program, and should have used the 'autoshape' facility.

Key background information

This activity builds on 'Planet of the shapes' (page 47), and combines the technique of using autoshapes with freehand painting on the screen. It is best undertaken in the context of work on a related subject, such as life cycles in science.

Preparation

Prepare a help sheet that shows the position of the power switch, disk drive and so on. Include a step-by-step guide to loading the program. Photocopiable page 120 can be used as a basis for this. This sheet can be kept near the computer for reference during this and other activities.

Resources needed

An art program with the 'autoshape' option, a colour printer, a help sheet (see 'Preparation').

INFORMATION TECHNOLOGY

What to do

Start with the computer switched off and demonstrate how to load up the program, talking through the process. If possible, encourage the children to conceptualise what is going on: the idea of the hard disk as a 'library', from which you can take items you want to use, is often helpful. The analogy can be continued with the program being opened up and used like a book, then returned when you have finished with it.

Remind the children about the range of painting tools available in the program, discussing when to use thin or thick markers and so on. Use the 'fill' tool to create a green or blue background as a basis for an 'underwater' picture. Drawing on the children's suggestions, build up the picture using various techniques. Discuss how they could add air bubbles using the circle shape. Before your picture is complete, discuss why you might want to save it; asking the children to guide you, demonstrate how to save the file.

Organise the children into pairs and set the task: to create an underwater picture using the range of painting tools, the 'autoshapes' and any other techniques they may be familiar with. They should attempt to load the program and save their pictures independently. Refer them to the help sheet (see 'Preparation') if appropriate.

Suggestions for extension

More confident children can be led to use a wider range of painting tools by appropriate suggestions, such as 'Can you draw ripples in the water?' (using *colour wash*) or 'Can you draw an octopus with a cloud of ink?' (using *paint spray*). They should be encouraged to print out their work independently.

Suggestion(s) for support

Some children will need to be supported when loading the program and saving their finished pictures. They may need to repeat the operation several times, so try to allow some time for them to practise loading and saving, gradually reducing the amount of help given.

Assessment opportunities

This activity can be used to assess the extent to which children can work independently. Particular attention should be given to switching on, loading up and starting work without adult support. The more the children are able to do this, the more time you will have to support their learning rather than organising the hardware and software for them.

Display ideas

The finished pictures could be used as covers or title pages for relevant topic books or folders, or combined (as a wall display) with a table display about shore life.

Reference to photocopiable sheet.

Photocopiable page 120 is a 'blank' help sheet which can be filled in with appropriate instructions for the particular system being used.

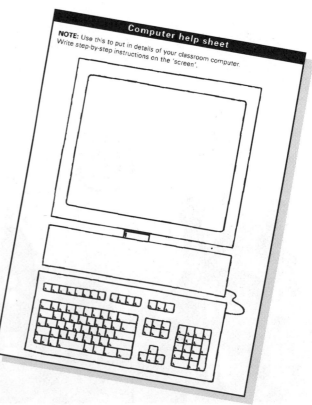

INFORMATION TECHNOLOGY

LIGHT AND SHADE

To develop mouse skills further. To develop skills in freehand drawing using painting tools. To load a program, save and print out with increasing independence.

†† *Whole-class discussion; activity in groups of 3.*

🕐 *10–15 minutes discussion/demonstration time; 30–45 minutes computer time.*

Previous skills/knowledge needed

The children need to be familiar with an art program, and be able to use the 'fill' facility. They should have drawn silhouettes of facial profiles in the conventional way, using a torch to cast a shadow of a child's face.

Key background information

This activity should follow plenty of experience in pattern making and the use of autoshapes and 'stamps' (or 'motifs'). It is best undertaken in the context of line drawing activities in art. Painting with light on a computer screen is very different from painting with a brush on paper, and requires very good skill in mouse control. This activity is simple in the sense that there is only one line to draw; but practice will be needed before the children are satisfied with the result.

Language to be introduced

Silhouette, erasing, cutting out, zoom, consultant.

Preparation

Ask the children each to bring in a small cardboard photograph frame (of the kind normally supplied by school photographers). Alternatively, they could make their own frames as a design and technology activity. Make sure that some silhouettes from the children's previous art or science work are available to be examined.

Resources needed

An art program with the 'fill' facility, a black and white (or colour) printer, a torch or overhead projector, suitable wall areas for shadow silhouettes to be made, examples of silhouettes from previous work.

What to do

Refer to previous work on drawing silhouettes, and look at some examples with the class. Introduce the idea of using the computer to produce miniature silhouettes. Explain how art programs generally allow a smaller version of a picture to be created, either on the screen or by printing out on a smaller scale.

With the help of two children (one as 'model' and one to operate the projector or hold the torch), demonstrate how to copy the shadow image which falls on a projector screen using the painting tool on the computer screen. Make the image fill the whole screen, and encourage the children to do the same. Once you have produced a basic outline, make improvements to the image by using the 'eraser' on the screen. When the outline is satisfactory, fill the face profile in black to produce a conventional silhouette.

INFORMATION
TECHNOLOGY

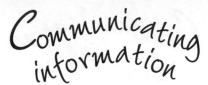

Try alternative colours and invite the children's comments. Next, show them how to make the image smaller by 'cutting out' and resizing or by using the 'zoom' facility.

Organise the children into groups of three and set the task: to create a shadow silhouette of each child on the projector screen and recreate it on the computer screen. Remind the children of the importance of co-operation and mutual support. If possible, allow some time before they use the computer for them to practise and refine the production of actual shadow silhouettes. This will save time when it is their turn on the computer. Specify the amount of time allowed for each of the three children in the group to produce a silhouette on screen. To save time, it may be useful to save the images and print them out later; encourage the children to do this independently, if possible. Designate some children as 'IT consultants' for this activity (see 'Introduction', page 6).

If the children have brought in cardboard photograph frames or have made their own, help them to make sure that their final prints are the right size to fit these frames.

Suggestions for extension
More confident children may wish to try altering the completed image. For example, by using the cut and paste facility, multiple shadows could be created in different colours.

Suggestion(s) for support
Try to ensure that less confident children each work with two more confident ones. Check that the 'IT consultants' are providing support when required.

Assessment opportunities
This activity can be used to assess how well children can control the mouse to achieve a particular image, rather than an abstract effect. Also, by observing the process, you may be able to judge how confident children are in using the eraser, changing colours, making a fresh start and so on.

Display ideas
The children's printed and framed silhouettes could be displayed with labels inviting people to guess who is portrayed in each silhouette.

SPRAY THAT AGAIN!

To be introduced to the 'paint spray' facility and practise using it.

†† *Whole-class discussion; paired activity.*

🕐 *15 minutes discussion/demonstration time; 30 minutes computer time.*

Previous skills/knowledge needed
The children need to have reasonable confidence in using a painting program, and should be able to select tools and colours.

INFORMATION
TECHNOLOGY

Key background information

Most painting programs have a 'paint spray' facility. This is often depicted on the toolbar as a picture of a spray can with paint emerging from it. When selected, this produces a spray effect on the screen in the current colour. The size of the spray can usually be adjusted to allow very fine spraying. This tool allows subtle changes to be made to existing colours; it can also be used to paint rain, smoke and so on.

Language to be introduced

Paint spray, colour wash.

Preparation

You will need some clip art pictures to which clouds, smoke or spray could be added – for example, a train, a factory or a ship. Obtain some prints or postcards of atmospheric landscapes or seascapes by Turner (or a similar artist).

Resources needed

A painting program with the 'paint spray' facility, a colour printer, suitable clip art pictures (see 'Preparation'), examples of painted landscapes or seascapes by Turner.

What to do

Demonstrate how to use the 'paint spray' to add a 'texture' effect to a picture, and to create smoke, steam or cloud. On a new page, build up a picture using only the spray tool, asking the children to suggest appropriate subjects. Demonstrate how to undo the last action on screen, and how to over-spray to change colours. Show the children some paintings by Turner, drawing attention to the large areas of colour and the subtle changes in shade and tone, and to the fact that there are very few distinct lines or boundaries.

Organise the children into pairs and set the task: to paint a picture using only the paint spray. Ask them to think of suitable subjects – such as hailstorms, fireworks, tidal waves or comets – while they are waiting for their turn at the computer, as this will give them more actual painting time.

Suggestion(s) for extension

Some children may wish to re-open an existing picture and use the spray tool to enhance it. Some paint programs have a 'colour wash' facility which replicates the effect of conventional colour washing: the more times you brush over an area, the deeper the colour becomes. The children could use this to transform pictures made using the normal range of colours – for example, turning a sunny day into a storm.

Suggestion(s) for support

Less confident children may need support in selecting the 'paint spray' tool and in using it boldly on the screen. Remind them that mistakes can always be corrected by using the 'undo' facility or by over-painting.

Assessment opportunities

This activity can be used to assess how well the children can achieve a spray action with the mouse. This skill requires quite subtle movements, and may take some time to be fully developed. The task is quite open-ended, so the assessment opportunities will depend on the children's response and your opportunities to observe them working.

Display ideas

The children's paintings could be used as a background to a display of work on a science theme such as 'Water' or 'Fire'. They could also be displayed alongside paintings by artists such as Turner, with a label asking the viewer to look for similarities.

INFORMATION TECHNOLOGY

FEARFUL SYMMETRY

To practise screen painting techniques in the context of representational art. To understand the advantages and disadvantages of using a computer rather than conventional media.

†† *Whole-class discussion; paired activity.*

⏰ *20 minutes discussion/demonstration time; 30 minutes computer time.*

Previous skills/knowledge needed

The children need to be confident in using a painting program, choosing brush sizes and colours as appropriate. They need competence in using most of the tools available, including fill, spray and erase/undo.

Key background information

Representational images are more difficult to achieve with a mouse than with a pencil or brush. This activity should follow plenty of practice in using the various techniques available in a paint program to achieve a satisfying effect. Making representational art the focus of an introductory activity can be highly discouraging for the child.

However, a major advantage of using the computer for painting is the fact that you can make as many attempts on the same 'canvas' as time allows. Infant children generally have a certain boldness in their approach to painting which is often diminished as they become older. Such an approach is well suited to painting with a computer, as the child's initial marks can be replaced or refined until he/she is happy with the picture.

Preparation

Obtain some prints or magazine pictures of wild and domestic animals. Prepare and save screen pages with outlines of animal faces.

Resources needed

A painting program with a range of facilities, a colour printer, printed pictures of animals, outlines of animal faces saved on disk, a large (flat) plastic-backed mirror (see 'Display ideas').

What to do

Within a suitable topic such as Animals, Pets or Growth, discuss the size and position of animal facial features. Show the children some pictures of domestic and/or wild animals. Point out the similarities and differences between different animals. *How symmetrical are the faces? How do they look when you place a mirror down the middle of each face: are both sides exactly the same?*

Remind the children of the facilities available in the painting program. Organise them into pairs and set the task:

to paint an animal's face on screen. If appropriate, refer them to photocopiable sheet 121, which contains a summary of the tools available in two common painting programs. Encourage the use of the spray tool to create a 'furry' effect. Demonstrate how to save a file, and suggest that they save their own pictures.

Suggestion(s) for extension

Although real faces are not perfectly symmetrical, some children may find it interesting to use the 'auto-symmetry' tool available in some painting programs. Some children may also be able to use the 'zoom' facility to refine their designs. For example, a highlight could be inserted into an eye by increasing the scale of the picture and adding a spot or two of white. When the picture is reduced back to its original size, it appears that a tiny fleck of light is reflected in the pupil.

Suggestion(s) for support

The mention of 'templates' is bound to draw disparaging remarks from many infant teachers. Nevertheless, some children may benefit from having the facial proportions of an animal marked out for them on the screen. Simply

INFORMATION TECHNOLOGY

making two marks to indicate the position of the eyes on a blank page might be enough to get less confident children started. The most important thing is for the face drawing to fill the screen: if the child starts by outlining a very small face, drawing and refining the features becomes far more difficult.

Encourage the children to experiment. Less confident children are often reluctant to make a start for fear of making mistakes. The computer has infinite 'patience', so emphasise this fact. Minor mistakes can be rectified quickly, or a completely fresh start can be made. You can act as a role model when demonstrating the program, so try to include some 'deliberate' mistakes as you go along.

Assessment opportunities

This activity can be used to assess how well the children can use a wide range of computer features and painting techniques. It could be used as a summative assessment task, following several sessions of work with a painting program. If so, close observation of and careful discussion with individual children will be necessary.

Display ideas

Include the finished animal pictures in the topic display. Alternatively, include them in a display about symmetry and ask the children to say whether each picture has exact line symmetry. A large, flat plastic-backed mirror could be made available for children to test the pictures and any other shapes included in the display.

YES, THAT'S ME WITH THE PARACHUTE

To extend screen painting techniques in the context of representational art. To understand further the advantages and disadvantages of using a computer rather than conventional media. To be introduced to 'clip art' and practise saving and retrieving images on disk.

†† *Whole-class discussion; paired activity.*

🕐 *15 minutes discussion/demonstration time; 20 minutes and 10 minutes computer time.*

Darren

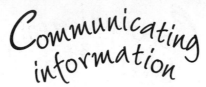

Previous skills/knowledge needed
The children need to have confidence in using a painting program, and be able to select brush sizes and colours. They should be competent in using most of the tools available, including fill, spray and erase/undo.

Key background information
See 'Fearful symmetry' (page 53) for notes on using a computer to paint representational images.

'Clip art' is a generic term for images that have been created and saved on disk. Most computer packages include some clip art images, and all painting programs do so. These images can usually be found in a directory called 'clip art'.

Language to be introduced
Clip art.

Preparation
Prepare floppy disks with pages containing suitable clip art images, or copy these into a particular directory on the hard disk. This makes them easier to find. Using an art package, prepare an image of yourself and save it on disk. Make one copy per child of photocopiable page 121 (if appropriate).

Resources needed
A painting program with a range of facilities, a colour printer, an appropriate range of clip art images, photocopiable page 121 (if appropriate); an image of yourself, saved on disk.

What to do
Within a suitable topic such as 'Ourselves', discuss the children's activities outside school. Ask them to say what activities they would like to do; encourage imaginative and fantastic ideas. Introduce the children to the notion of 'clip art', and demonstrate how to preview an image and how to insert it into the current page of the painting program. Demonstrate how the image can be modified using the familiar painting tools.

Explain the task: for each child to choose a piece of clip art and add to it a picture of her/himself. For example, the child could be the pilot of a plane, the lion tamer in a circus or a skier in a downhill race. Demonstrate this process by adding your own picture to the clip art image on screen. Now demonstrate how to save work in progress, and explain that you are going to use this activity to see how independently they can save and retrieve their pictures.

Organise pairings and devise a rota to give each pair two computer sessions: 10 minutes to get started, then 20 minutes to complete the picture. This requires them to carry out the saving and opening techniques successfully. If appropriate, refer them to photocopiable sheet 121, which contains a summary of the tools available in two common painting programs.

If you have access to a scanner, photographs of the children could be scanned in for inclusion in the finished pictures. A digital camera is ideal for this purpose, since it allows photographic images to be transferred directly to the computer. However, most children will probably be content to generate self-portraits using the facilities of the paint program.

Suggestion(s) for extension
Children with a good level of skill should be encouraged to explore any clip art files which are available. If they find images relating to their current work in any area of the curriculum, they could be encouraged to incorporate these into their word processing.

Suggestion(s) for support
Some children are likely to need help in saving and retrieving their work. Parents and other volunteers will obviously be useful in this respect; or you could appoint more confident children to be 'IT Consultants' for the class (see the Introduction on page 6).

Assessment opportunities
This activity can be used to assess the children's level of independence in saving and retrieving their work. If it is used in this way, close observation of and/or careful discussion with individual children will be necessary.

Display ideas
The children's completed pictures

Zoth

could be displayed under a heading such as 'Our hobbies' or 'What we did at the weekend'.

Reference to photocopiable sheet

Photocopiable page 121 contains a summary of the tools available in two common painting programs. If the information matches the program being used, this sheet will be useful when the children are carrying out the activity.

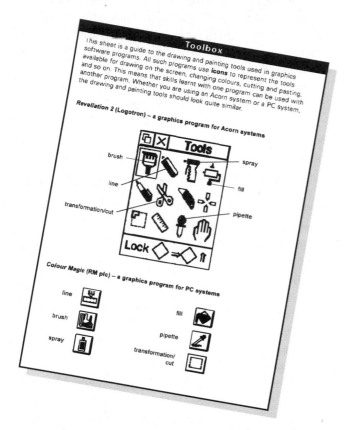

THREE BLIND MICE

To be introduced to the idea of representing musical phrases by pictures. To know the techniques for playing individual phrases and for creating a musical sequence (using the 'drag and drop' technique).

†† *Whole class.*

🕐 *30–45 minutes.*

Previous skills/knowledge needed

The children do not need any particular computer skills for this activity, as the teacher operates the computer. They should be able to distinguish between musical phrases.

Key background information

The 'Communicating and handling information' strand of IT in the National Curriculum includes the communication of ideas in sound. In the exemplar material, specific reference is made to using pictures on screen to represent musical phrases. This allows children to access phrases – and use them as 'musical building blocks' when composing tunes – without being able to read standard notation. The pictures used are arbitrary and simply identify the different phrases. They are not in any sense related to 'graphic notation' for music. Most programs have files of familiar tunes, such as 'Three Blind Mice' and 'The Teddy Bears' Picnic'; when such a file is loaded, the relevant bank of pictures appears on the screen.

The *Compose World* screen has two 'windows' or 'boxes'. One contains eight or more pictures, each representing a particular musical phrase. To listen to each phrase, you select the picture with the pointer and click with the mouse. The other box has sixteen blank spaces arranged as 4 x 4 (this format can be altered), as well as *play, stop, pause* and other controls which are operated by mouse clicks. The tune is built up by 'dragging' pictures from the bank of phrases to the sequencer grid and 'dropping' them in place as required. The speed of the tune can be altered. The other controls operate very much as for a conventional cassette player. The next five activities provide an introduction to this kind of composition and performance which is suitable for children at Key Stage 1, or for older children who have had no previous experience of using this kind of software.

Although it is not essential for introductory activities, the use of a MIDI (Musical Industry Digital Interface) to connect a musical keyboard to the computer will greatly enhance the sound quality. If you are using a 'multimedia' computer, this will also be able to produce realistic instrumental sounds.

Language to be introduced

Musical phrase, tune, drag and drop, select, listen, play, stop.

What to do

Gather the children around the computer. Use the tune file to play the phrases of 'Three Blind Mice' (or a similar tune) in a random order. Ask the children whether any of the phases sound familiar. *Do they remind you of a particular tune? Which phrase is at the beginning? What comes next?* Work with the children until the phrases have been correctly ordered into the complete tune. Ask the children whether they noticed the technique you used to choose a phrase so that you could hear what it sounded like before placing it in the sequence. Repeat this technique several times, and ask for volunteers to try it out. Tell them that next time they will be using the program themselves, so they need to remember what you have shown them.

(Because this session is an introductory teacher demonstration, there are no suggestions for extension, support or assessment.)

Preparation

Make sure that you are familiar with the software beforehand – particularly the way in which phrases are played and are moved around the screen to create a sequence (see 'Key background information'). Load the tune file for 'Three Blind Mice' (or a similar tune), so that the pictures representing the musical phases it contains are displayed.

Resources needed

A computer with a program that uses pictures to represent musical phrases (such as *Compose World* or *Compose World Junior*, published by ESP), a tune file for a well-known song.

THE TEDDY BEARS' PICNIC

To practise the techniques for playing individual phrases, and for creating a musical sequence using the 'drag and drop' technique.

†† *Whole-class discussion; activity in pairs or small groups.*

🕐 *15–20 minutes discussion/demonstration time; 30 minutes computer time.*

Previous skills/knowledge needed

The children need to be reasonably confident in using the mouse to move the pointer around the screen and to select, drag and drop. They should have been introduced to the music software being used, and should understand the use of pictures to represent musical phrases.

Key background information

See 'Three Blind Mice' on page 56.

INFORMATION TECHNOLOGY

pictures/phrases. As you play the phrases, encourage the children to listen carefully for any that sound familiar. When they have identified the phrases as those making up 'The Teddy Bears' Picnic', tell them that their task is to arrange the musical phrases into the correct sequence. Organise them into pairs or threes and devise a rota for computer work.

As each group completes the activity, listen to the tune to check that the sequence is correct.

Suggestion(s) for extension
The phrases which make up the tune might still produce an acceptable tune if they were arranged differently. If time permits, the more confident children might like to experiment with different sequences.

Suggestion(s) for support
Careful grouping can provide support for those children who have difficulty in distinguishing between the different phrases, or who are not confident in the techniques required to play the phrases and arrange them in a sequence. If appropriate, a simpler tune such as 'Three Blind Mice' (which was used in the original demonstration) could be used here.

Assessment opportunities
As you listen to the finished sequences, ask individual children to demonstrate the techniques for playing phrases and adding them to the sequence. Note their level of confidence.

Performance ideas
The children in each group could sing along with the completed tune as they play it to the class. Each group could play and sing the tune at a different tempo.

Language to be introduced
Musical phrase, tune, drag and drop, select, listen, play, stop (as for 'Three Blind Mice').

Preparation
Load up the tune file for 'The Teddy Bears' Picnic' (or a similar tune), so that the pictures representing the musical phrases this tune contains are displayed on screen. For this activity, the computer will need to be kept in a place where the sound of music (as each group carries out the task) is unlikely to disturb the rest of the class. Headphones will be useful only if the children are working individually, since two or more people wearing them tend to shout at each other.

Resources needed
A computer with a program (such as *Compose World* or *Compose World Junior*) that uses pictures to represent musical phrases.

What to do
This activity should follow the demonstration described in 'Three Blind Mice' (page 56). Remind the children of this demonstration, and ask them whether they remember how to play musical phrases and how to build up a sequence. Ask for volunteers to direct you around the current set of

---

IF YOU'RE HAPPY AND YOU KNOW IT

To practise further the techniques for playing individual phrases and for creating a musical sequence.

†† *Whole-class discussion; paired or small-group activity.*

🕐 *20 minutes discussion/demonstration time; 30 minutes computer time.*

Previous skills/knowledge needed
The children should have used a music program, and be familiar with the techniques for playing phrases and for making them into a sequence.

Key background information

See 'Three Blind Mice' on page 56. Following activities which involve using known tunes, this activity involves composing new ones. The musical phrases in a tune file are written so that each phrase can follow any other (see Figure 8). However, arranging them at random will not usually result in a satisfactory tune. This activity requires the children to select particular phrases in relation to their suitability for starting, continuing or ending a line. Although many phrases can be used at the beginning or in the middle of a sequence, only certain phrases will sound 'right' at the end of a sequence (in musical terms, 'resolving' the tune successfully). It is not necessary for the children to understand this principle in musical terms; but most children should be able to tell intuitively whether or not a sequence of phrases 'sounds right'. Figure 9 shows a typical 'tune' sequence of phrases on screen.

The key in which each bank or file of phrases is written

can suggest a particular mood. A tune file is written in a major or a minor key, which is usually – but not necessarily – associated with a happy or more melancholy mood respectively.

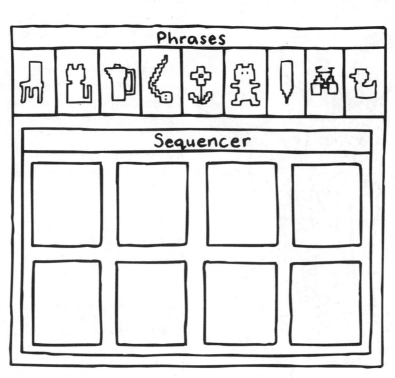

Figure 8

Language to be introduced

Mood, major key, minor key.

Preparation

See 'Three Blind Mice' on page 56. From the range of tune files available, identify some which would be useful for composing 'happy' tunes.

Resources needed

A computer with a program that uses pictures to represent musical phrases.

What to do

Remind the children of their previous work, when they arranged musical phrases in a pre-determined sequence to play a familiar tune. Remind them of the techniques for selecting and sequencing phrases. Select a tune file (see 'Preparation') and play each phrase in turn, asking the children whether they think the phrase sounds

Figure 9

INFORMATION TECHNOLOGY

Suggestion(s) for extension

More confident children can be encouraged to explore the facilities of the program. They may wish to change the standard format of four lines with four phrases each. The program allows the 'layout' – the number of rows and columns – to be customised. Some children may be able to save their own compositions.

Suggestion(s) for support

Make sure that children needing support work with someone who is more confident. If possible, provide adult support and/or allow more time at the computer.

Assessment opportunities

Children who are able to compose a tune with a good degree of independence will have attained at least Level 2 in IT.

Performance ideas

See 'Join the band', page 61.

FROM MAJOR TO MINOR

To practise further the techniques for playing individual phrases and for creating a musical sequence. To know how to change the speed of a tune.

†† *Whole-class discussion; paired or small-group activity.*

🕐 *20 minutes discussion/demonstration time; 30 minutes computer time.*

---

like a 'beginning, middle or end'. Following their suggestions, compose a sequence which everyone is satisfied with as a tune.

Show them how to repeat a line (made up of four phrases) when composing a tune; and how to repeat a line except for the final phrase. Draw attention to the use of this format in familiar tunes, such as 'If You're Happy and You Know It', 'Three Blind Mice' and 'The Teddy Bears' Picnic'. *Which parts of the tune are the same? Which are different?*

Organise the children into pairs or threes and devise a rota for them to use the program. Tell them which tune files to choose from when they take their turn at the computer, and explain that they are to compose 'cheerful' or 'upbeat' tunes. Ask them to let you know when their compositions are finished, so that you can save them for everyone to listen to later.

When all the pairs or groups have completed a composition, play them back. Ask the rest of the class to comment on the pieces.

Previous skills/knowledge needed

The children should have used the music program, and be familiar with the techniques for playing phrases and for making them into a sequence. This activity should also follow 'If You're Happy and You Know It' (page 58).

Key background information

See 'If You're Happy and You Know It'. The key in which each bank or file of phrases is written can suggest a particular mood (major for 'happy' tunes, minor for 'sad' or 'peaceful' ones). Changing the speed or tempo of a piece can also dramatically alter the mood.

Language to be introduced

Mood, major key, minor key, tempo.

Resources needed

A computer with a program (such as *Compose World* or *Compose World Junior*) that uses pictures to represent musical phrases.

Preparation

See 'Three Blind Mice' on page 56. From the range of tune files available, identify some which would be useful for composing melancholy tunes rather than bright and cheerful ones.

What to do

Remind the children of the previous activity, in which they composed their own 'cheerful' tunes. Recap the techniques for selecting phrases and ordering them into a sequence. Select a tune file (see 'Preparation') and play some phrases, asking the children to listen out for phrases which sound like a 'beginning, middle or end'. Following their suggestions, compose a tune that all the children are satisfied with.

Next, change the speed of the tune you have just composed. Introduce the word *tempo*. *What difference does this make? Which is the most appropriate tempo for this tune? What images does the music bring to mind: a quiet night in a forest, a sleepy summer's day, a lonely seagull flying over the sea?* Tell the children that you want them to compose a tune with a 'peaceful' or 'downbeat' theme. Show them how to change the tempo.

Organise the children into pairs or threes and devise a rota for them to use the program. Ask them to let you know when their compositions are finished, so that you can save them for everyone to listen to later.

When all the pairs or groups have completed a composition, play them back. Ask the rest of the class to suggest the mood of each piece, and ask the composers to say what their intentions were. *What pictures were you trying to convey in the music?*

Suggestion(s) for extension

More confident children can be encouraged to explore the facilities of the program. They may wish to change the standard format of four lines with four phrases each. The program allows the 'layout' – the number of rows and columns – to be customised. Some children may be able to save their own compositions.

Suggestion(s) for support

Make sure that children needing support work with someone who is more confident. If possible, provide adult support and/or allow more time at the computer.

Assessment opportunities

Children who can compose a tune independently will have attained at least Level 2 in IT.

Performance ideas

See 'Join the band' below.

JOIN THE BAND

To develop an understanding of how computers are integrated into many forms of music. To use the computer alongside conventional instruments for performing compositions.

†† *Whole class or groups.*

🕐 . *Open-ended discussion and performance time.*

Previous skills/knowledge needed

The children should have composed tunes, and these should have been saved on disk. They should be reasonably competent in playing unpitched percussion instruments and following the directions of a conductor.

Key background information

See 'Three Blind Mice' (page 56), 'If You're Happy and You Know It' (page 58) and 'From major to minor' (page 60).

Almost all recorded music, in any genre, involves the use of a computer. Electronically-generated rhythm tracks and 'samples' (sounds recorded from another piece of music and stored on a computer in digital form) are frequently used alongside conventional instruments during performance and recording. This activity is designed to extend the children's understanding of the use of IT in everyday life, and to provide a suitable conclusion to their

INFORMATION
TECHNOLOGY

previous composition work.

If a MIDI keyboard is available, this can be connected to the computer. Tunes can then be played back in a variety of 'voices': instrumental modes such as strings, saxophone and piano. It also allows more control over volume, allowing children to turn up the volume of the music from the computer so that they can hear it while they are playing instruments. Alternatively, speakers can be added to the computer system for more volume. Multimedia systems also have a 'sound-card' which allows music to be played in different 'voices' and the volume to be adjusted.

Language to be introduced
Percussion, rhythm, pulse, tempo, conductor.

Preparation
Make sure that the children's compositions are readily accessible on disk. If possible, arrange to use a computer which will allow the tunes to be played through a good-quality sound system, such as a multimedia system or MIDI keyboard. Acquire a range of percussion instruments such as drums, cymbals and maracas. Obtain some recordings which combine computer-generated sounds with conventional instruments, such as 'house' or 'techno' dance music or electronic pop music (Bowie, Eno and so on).

Resources needed
A computer with a program that uses pictures to represent musical phrases, files of the children's own musical compositions from previous activities, a range of percussion instruments, recordings of partly computer-generated music (see 'Preparation'), a MIDI keyboard (if available).

What to do
Depending on the children's general level of confidence and competence in playing percussion instruments, allow some time for them to practise playing and following your direction as 'conductor'.

Play back a composition and ask the children to suggest appropriate percussion accompaniments. Play back the tune several more times, so that the children can practise and refine their performance. Encourage them to suggest changes in the volume and tempo of the playback. When they know what they are doing, ask them to organise the playback of their recording, making any appropriate changes to it as they go along. Repeat this with as many different tunes as the time allows, trying to make sure that a variety of different tune files and types of composition are included. If possible, record the performances on cassette.

Following this, discuss with the children how computers are often combined with conventional instruments when pop records are made. Play some examples, asking the children to distinguish between the computer-generated sounds and the conventional instruments.

Suggestion(s) for extension
Some children could be encouraged to write lyrics for their compositions using a word processor. (See 'Wax lyrical' on page 36.)

Assessment opportunities
When the children are asked to organise the playback of their recording, note how successfully they use the techniques for starting, stopping, changing between tempos and so on.

Performance ideas
The children could play the tunes, with their own live accompaniment, during a class or school assembly (or as part of a concert).

Handling information

The activities in this section show children how to use IT as a means of collecting, sorting and displaying data. The children should be aware of the purpose served by collecting the information, and should be introduced to the idea that conclusions may be drawn from particular patterns in the data. At Key Stage 1, many everyday contexts can be used to introduce work on handling information.

Children are not expected to be able to create a database until Key Stage 2. However, in helping the teacher to build up a database with the information they have collected, children should develop an understanding of the process. Some may be able to create a simple database independently.

This section also contains two activities which involve working with CD-ROMs. The 'encyclopaedia' type of CD-ROM, which contains lots of information that children can explore, provides excellent opportunities for extending their experience of handling information. Accessing information from such a source is perfectly feasible at Key Stage 1. However, care should be taken to ensure both that the children know how to find relevant information and that they can use it appropriately. They need to be given specific tasks which involve more than simply copying large passages of text verbatim. Directed Activities Related to the Text (DARTs) can be used successfully in this context (see *Curriculum Bank Reading Key Stage 1*: 'Evaluating information books', page 102).

INFORMATION
TECHNOLOGY

SIX SNAKES, FOUR FERRETS

To know how a computer can be used to collect, sort and display information. To begin to interpret data.

†† *Whole class.*

🕑 *20 minutes discussion/demonstration time.*

Previous skills/knowledge needed

Before they explore the use of a computer to generate graphs, it is essential for the children to have plenty of experience in gathering information and representing it pictorially. For example, matchboxes could be used to produce simple bar graphs showing how many children have their birthdays in each month or have particular numbers of brothers and sisters. Activities with the computer should be seen as an integral part of this work.

Key background information

The term *database* refers to any set of information that is organised in a systematic way. In this activity, the information relates to pets; organising this data under specific headings produces a database. In this case, only one heading or *field* is used. If the data were categorised into (for example) pets which were more/less than 15cm high or pets which had two/four/no legs, then 'height' and 'number of legs' would become additional fields. Data handling activities at Key Stage 2 involve 'searching' fields – for example, looking for all those pets which have four legs and are below 15cm in height. This is known as a *logical search*.

When you are collecting data with the children, it is important that the information is expressed in an unambiguous way. For example, in response to the question *How many of you have a cat?* some children might put two hands up to indicate that they have two cats. An early emphasis on clarity and precision will pay dividends later, when the children are collecting data independently and tackling more complicated work with databases.

Software designed for this age group usually has the facility to generate graphs as the information is entered: as categories or fields are entered and assigned a numerical value, a column-shaped block appears in an adjacent window. Demonstrating this reinforces the concept that the computer can carry out operations in a split second.

If your computer has the program *Pictogram* (available from Kudliansoft), this will allow you to produce pictograms instead of bar charts. A pictogram involves the repetition of an image as a unit; the images in different columns may be selected as different versions of the same picture (see Figure 1b) or as different pictures (see Figure 1a).

Language to be introduced

Information, bar chart, pie chart, database.

Resources needed

A computer with a program which can generate bar charts and pie charts from lists of data, such as *DataSweet*, *Datashow* or *Information Workshop* (see the Resources list on pages 142 and 143).

What to do

Within the context of work on Animals, Pets or Ourselves, gather the children around the computer and discuss their pets. Ask how many of them have a cat, a dog and so on; enter the categories and respective totals into the program. Point out the relationship between the totals and the length of the bars which are generated as you enter the information.

When you have a complete bar chart on screen, ask literal questions about it, such as: *How many more children have a pet*

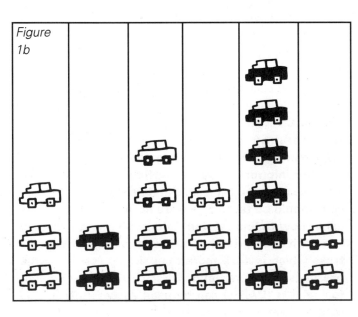

Figure 1a

Figure 1b

INFORMATION
TECHNOLOGY

dog than a pet rabbit? Encourage the children to ask and answer similar questions for themselves. It is also important to discuss inferential interpretations of the data – that is, insights into how the data might be explained. Inferential questions such as *Why do you think more children have fish than dogs?* and *Why do you think only one person has a parrot?* can develop the children's understanding of statistics and provide a good basis for subsequent work.

Even at this level, the children can begin to predict that the graph would look similar if the same information were collected from a parallel class. It is important that they see the bar chart not as an end-product, but as a step in the process of thinking about the information.

The same information can often (depending on the program) be displayed on screen as a pie chart. Like a bar chart, a pie chart can be generated automatically from the data by selecting it from the range of available graph types. If possible, contrast the bar chart and pie chart versions of the data. Draw attention to the way in which the size of each piece of the 'pie' reflects a proportion of the total data collected.

As a follow-up activity, the children can be given a printout of the bar chart with some questions to answer individually. Provide a mixture of literal and inferential questions, for example:
▲ *Which is the most popular kind of pet?*
▲ *Why does only one person have a pony?*
▲ *Which kind of pet do you think is the easiest to look after?*

Suggestion(s) for extension
More confident pupils can be asked to respond verbally to inferential questions.

Suggestion(s) for support
The questions accompanying the bar chart can be differentiated to match the ability of the children. Less confident children could be asked only literal questions.

Assessment opportunities
During the discussion, note those children who understand the relationship between the original data and the bar chart. Note those children who can answer literal questions, and those who offer ideas in response to inferential questions. Look out for answers that include references to the difficulty or expenses of looking after certain pets, or for those which suggest that results from a parallel class might be similar. Some children may be developing an understanding of the notion of likelihood.

Display ideas
The completed bar chart and pie chart could be displayed together with captions suggested by the children.

TRAFFIC JAM

To know how a computer can be used to collect, sort and display information. To develop further ability to interpret data.

✛ *Whole-class discussion; activity in small groups.*

🕐 *45 minutes discussion/demonstration time; time for collecting data at intervals during the day.*

Previous skills/knowledge needed
The children should have been introduced to a simple database program which produces bar charts as information is entered. See 'Six snakes, four ferrets' on page 64.

Language to be introduced

Sort, period of time, tally chart.

Preparation

Make sure that the children know the rules for outdoor work. They must stay within the school grounds for this activity and be appropriately supervised. Although they will not be working directly at the side of the road, remind them that they should not distract drivers in any way. Also, they should not try this activity outside school, except perhaps from a window of their home.

Make one or two copies per child of the 'Traffic survey' data collection sheet (photocopiable page 122), depending on how many surveys they are going to carry out.

Resources needed

A computer with a program which can generate bar charts and pie charts from lists of data (see page 64), photocopiable page 122, a timer (optional) such as a 15-minute sand timer or a stopwatch.

What to do

In the context of work on 'Where we live' or 'Transport', introduce the idea of carrying out a traffic survey – if possible, using a road which is visible from the school. To whom would the information be useful? How could we collect the information? Introduce the idea of a tally chart and practise with some sample data, using conventional tally marks to record facts such as birthday months or means of travel to school. Discuss the usefulness of tally charts as a means of recording information quickly – particularly when you are watching events and keeping a record of what you see.

Ask the children what types of vehicle are likely to pass along the chosen road (for example, in the traffic going past the school gate). Write these vehicle names on the board and draw simple pictures next to them. Next, distribute copies of photocopiable page 122. Ask the children to copy down the vehicle names on the sheet and draw their own pictures in the appropriate spaces.

When they have prepared their sheets, take the children to a suitable observation point and help them to record different kinds of traffic for a specific length of time (such as 15 minutes). A timer or stopwatch might be useful for this, enabling the children to time themselves.

Back in the classroom, compare the children's results. Stress the need for careful recording. Enter the data into the graph drawing program and generate a bar chart. Discuss the completed graph, using similar questions to those suggested in 'Six snakes, four ferrets' (page 64). Include inferential questions such as 'What might the graph look like if we recorded the data at 8.30am instead of 10.00am?'

If the children can safely collect data from inside the school grounds, set up a rota for them to work in small groups to record the traffic flow in various 15-minute phases during the day. Provide new blank 'Traffic survey' sheets for this purpose. Adult supervision will be necessary, unless a suitable road can be watched from within the school building. Enter the data collected by the groups into the database.

When the information has been gathered, remind the

children how to enter the data and set up a rota for them to do this. Help them to print out copies of their bar charts. Discuss the differences in the volume and variety of traffic between different times of day. Ask the children to predict what the bar chart might look like at the same time of day on another weekday or a weekend day (choose the contrasting days in relation to local traffic patterns).

Suggestion(s) for extension

More confident children may be able to devise their own investigation, such as monitoring the movement along a particular corridor or the use of the school library. Pairs of children could be asked to produce an appropriate tally chart which includes all the likely categories of people, to collect and enter the data into the computer, and to print out a bar chart.

Suggestion(s) for support

Less confident children could work with the support of more confident children; or they could work together and be given specific adult help with gathering information, entering it into the computer and printing bar charts.

Assessment opportunities

Note how the children approach each stage of the activity. Pay particular attention to how accurately they record data using the tally chart, and their level of independence when entering the data into the computer.

Display ideas

In order to reinforce the use of graphs to present information, the bar charts could be displayed alongside similar graphs from newspapers and magazines. They could also be incorporated into a display on the risks of excessive traffic.

Reference to photocopiable sheet

Photocopiable page 122 is a blank 'Traffic survey' form for entering categories (types of vehicle) and recording tally marks and totals.

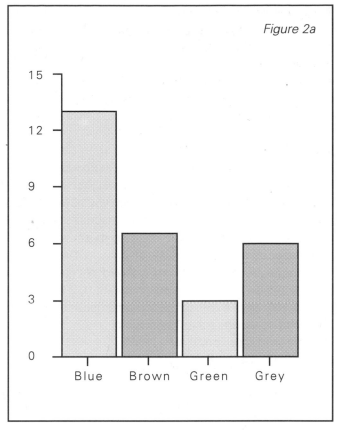

Figure 2a

it into a simple database in order to produce bar charts and pie charts – see 'Traffic jam' on page 65.

Key background information

This activity is designed to develop and assess the children's level of independence in gathering information and producing bar charts and pie charts on a computer.

SHAMPOO AND SET

To develop independence in collecting data and using a computer to display it as a bar chart or pie chart.

†† *Whole-class discussion; paired activity.*

🕐 *20 minutes discussion/demonstration time; 30 minutes computer time.*

Previous skills/knowledge needed

The children need to have collected data and to have entered

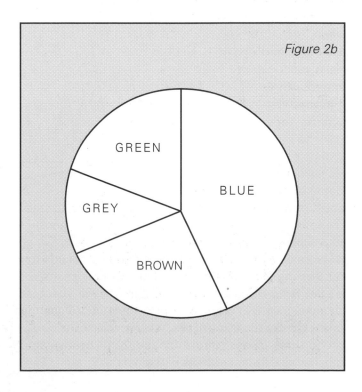

Figure 2b

Preparation
Make one copy of the 'Hair colour survey' sheet (photocopiable page 123) per child.

Resources needed
A computer with a program which can produce bar charts and pie charts from lists of data, photocopiable page 123.

What to do
In the context of work on 'Ourselves', introduce the idea of carrying out a survey into hair colour. Discuss previous information handling activities in which you have provided direction and support, and set the children the task of producing a bar chart or pie diagram to show accurate information about the distribution of hair colour in your class (or another class). Make sure that the children have a common understanding of what is meant by *blonde*, *dark brown*, *light brown* and so on, using particular children as examples to illustrate these definitions.

Through discussion, establish what the relevant categories of hair colour are. Write down the agreed colours and display them for the children to refer to during the activities. Tell them that you are going to see whether they can carry out the task with very little help. Ask children seated next to each other to work together in pairs, and – if they can see everyone from where they are – to stay in their seats while collecting the data. Distribute the data collection sheets (photocopiable page 123); ask the children to enter the agreed hair colours in the appropriate column, and then to complete the tally chart and count up the totals.

Once the pairs have recorded the raw data, set up a rota for them to use the computer to produce bar charts and pie diagrams. Discuss with the children whether a bar chart or a pie chart is more useful; help them to see that bar charts display actual quantities, whereas pie charts display proportions. (See Figures 2a and 2b.) The two thus emphasise different aspects of the data.

Suggestion(s) for extension
More confident children could be asked to collect and represent data about eye colour, devising their own categories. (Figures 2a and 2b show examples of 'eye colour' data charts.) Although this activity does not involve finding relationships between different sets of data, some children may notice a link between hair colour and eye colour.

Suggestion(s) for support
Less confident children could work with the support of more confident children; or they could work together and be given specific adult help with gathering information, entering it into the computer and printing bar/pie charts.

Assessment opportunities
The accuracy of the children's raw data can be checked and their level of independence monitored as pairs take their turn to enter information and produce bar charts and pie diagrams.

Display ideas
The bar and pie charts could be displayed alongside similar graphs from newspapers and magazines, to reinforce the use of graphs. They could also be incorporated into a display on 'Ourselves', introducing ideas about genetic diversity.

Reference to photocopiable sheet
Photocopiable page 123 is a blank 'Hair colour survey' form for entering categories (hair colours) and recording tally marks and totals.

INFORMATION TECHNOLOGY

DOWN AT HEEL

To practise collecting data and recording it on data collection sheets. To understand the need for accuracy. To see the relevance of information handling to everyday life. To work co-operatively.

†† *Whole-class discussion; paired activity.*

🕐 *20 minutes discussion/data collection time; 30 minutes computer time.*

Previous skills/knowledge needed

The children need to have collected data and to have entered it into a simple database in order to produce bar charts and pie charts – see 'Traffic Jam' (page 65) and 'Shampoo and Set' (page 67).

Key background information

As well as providing further experience of collecting and displaying data, this activity aims to develop the children's understanding of the relevance of data handling to everyday life. The emphasis is placed on the usefulness of the findings, rather than the method of presenting them.

Preparation

Make one copy per child of the 'Shoe size survey' data collection sheet (photocopiable page 124).

Resources needed

A computer with a program which can produce bar charts and pie charts from lists of data, photocopiable page 124, measuring equipment. A foot gauge (which could perhaps be borrowed from a shoe shop) and a chart giving the measurements of different shoe sizes would be useful.

What to do

In the context of work on 'Ourselves' or 'Growth', introduce the idea of collecting information about shoe sizes. Discuss previous information handling activities and how the data could be collected in this case. *Should everyone be asked their shoe size? Should everyone's shoes be examined to find indications of the size? Should everyone's feet be measured? What*

are the advantages and disadvantages of each strategy? Which is likely to be the most accurate?*

Set the children the task of collecting shoe size information from the whole class. This might be best achieved by asking each child in turn to tell everyone their shoe size, rather than have everyone talking at once or measuring one another's feet. Hand out copies of photocopiable page 124. The children should record each child's shoe size with a tally mark in the appropriate row of the data collection sheet, then add the marks to obtain the total for each size. Talk the children through the preparation of a database; and then choose individual children to enter each total into it. Set up a rota for pairs (or threes) to produce bar charts and pie diagrams using the computer.

Following this, discuss with the children who might benefit from having this information. Ask them what they think the graphs would look like if the information were collected from a younger or older class. It is not necessarily appropriate to include the idea of a *normal distribution* or a *bell-shaped curve* at this stage; but some children may notice that the central columns in the bar chart are taller than the outer ones.

Suggestion(s) for extension

More confident children could be shown how to copy a bar chart onto a page of text, using the 'cut and paste' technique. They could be asked to write some comments underneath the bar chart and to print out the page.

Suggestion(s) for support

Involve some less confident children in entering the data, with adult help.

Assessment opportunities

The final discussion should provide opportunities to assess the children's understanding of the reasons for using IT. Although the assessment of technical skills is relatively straightforward, insights into the development of knowledge and understanding are more difficult to acquire. Carefully-focused questions can help to build up a picture of children's capability in these aspects of the IT curriculum – for example:

▲ *What is the most/least common shoe size?*

▲ *How many children wear shoes bigger than size 1?*

▲ *Who might use this information?*

▲ *What do you think a graph of children's heights might look like?*

INFORMATION TECHNOLOGY

time (including am and pm), and be confident in reading an analogue clock face.

Key background information

This activity introduces the idea of *class intervals*, in which information is grouped together to make it easier to understand and use. For example, if you are recording the times at which different children go to bed, then 7.10pm, 7.20pm and 7.25pm might all be entered under the heading 7.00 – 7.29pm. This is an important concept for subsequent work in information handling. Although the children are not expected to decide on class intervals independently until they are working at a much higher level of mathematics, this activity provides appropriate experience in building up the concept.

Language to be introduced

Class interval.

Preparation

Write all the children's names on a large sheet of paper or a board. Enter the class intervals for recording bedtimes (see page 125) into an introductory database. Make copies (one of each per child) of photocopiable pages 125 and 126.

Resources needed

A computer with a program which can produce bar charts and pie charts from lists of data, photocopiable pages 125 and 126, clock faces (see 'Suggestion(s) for extension').

What to do

In the context of work on 'Time', 'Ourselves' or health education, introduce the idea of collecting information about bedtimes. Use the classroom clock to discuss time measurement if necessary. Ask the children to tell you individually what time they normally go to bed on a weekday evening. Enter each time against the appropriate name on the board or sheet of paper (see 'Preparation').

Distribute a copy of photocopiable page125 to each child. Ask them to record the bedtimes in the appropriate class interval boxes, using tally marks, and to count up the totals. When they have done this, discuss any patterns that have emerged. *Which is the most common half-hour period? Do many children go to bed relatively early or late?* (Be aware of children's possible sensitivity in these discussions.) Discuss who might use this information – for example, TV programme schedulers.

Next, remind the children of the labels given to the class intervals: 7–7.29 pm, 7.30–7.59 pm and so on. *What is the reason for ending each class interval with an unlikely time like 7.59 pm?* Set up a rota for the children, working in pairs, to enter the information into the computer and to produce bar charts and pie diagrams. Each pair should start a new database.

Display ideas

The bar/pie charts could be displayed alongside similar graphs from newspapers and magazines, to reinforce the use of graphs and introduce ideas about diversity and distribution. They could also be incorporated into a display on 'Feet', alongside silhouettes of shoe outlines and animal paw-prints.

Reference to photocopiable sheet

Photocopiable page 124 is a 'Shoe size survey' data collection sheet, with rows for entering categories and recording tally marks and totals.

UP THE WOODEN HILL

To collect numerical data and record it under class intervals.

†† *Whole-class discussion/data collection; paired computer work.*

🕐 *30 minutes discussion/data-collection time; 30 minutes computer time.*

Previous skills/knowledge needed

The children need to have collected data and to have entered it into a simple database in order to produce a selection of bar charts and pie diagrams – see 'Shampoo and set' on page 67 and 'Down at heel' on page 69. In addition, they will need to have a clear understanding of how to tell the

INFORMATION
TECHNOLOGY

Give out copies of the 'Data handling record sheet' (photocopiable page 126). Encourage each child to produce a graph independently, to be assessed by her/his partner. The partner can record on the sheet when this has been done successfully. This heightens their awareness of the skills involved in data handling.

Suggestion(s) for extension

The more confident children may be able to collect information about the length of time that different children spend in bed by finding out what time they go to bed and get up in the morning. If necessary, they can use clock faces to 'count on' by moving the hands from one time to another. They may find that bedtime alone is not an accurate indicator of how much sleep children get. This will help them to appreciate that sometimes recorded information does not tell you the whole story, and should be treated with caution.

Suggestion(s) for support

Some children may need more help in grasping the concept of class intervals, and in entering the data into the correct boxes in the table.

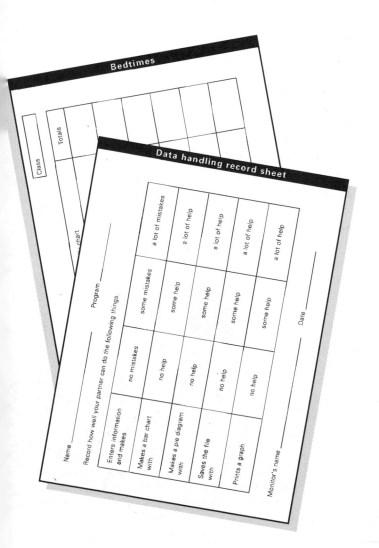

Assessment opportunities

Note how accurately the children enter the information into the computer. The children in each pair will assess one another's computer work, using the data handling record sheet (photocopiable page 126).

Display ideas

The bar charts and pie diagrams could be included as part of a general topic display. Printouts could be included in a *Bedtime Reading* book containing the children's accounts of their bedtime routines, favourite bedtime stories, teddy bear biographies and so on.

Reference to photocopiable sheets

Photocopiable page 125 is a 'Bedtimes' data collection sheet, with rows for recording bedtimes in half-hour class intervals. Photocopiable page 126 is a data handling record

INFORMATION TECHNOLOGY

sheet which the children in each pair can use to assess each other's computer work.

CHARTING SUCCESS

To choose an appropriate mode of display for data. To practise selecting from menu options and loading data files. To provide opportunities for teacher assessment of information-handling skills.

Whole-class discussion; paired activity.

15–20 minutes discussion time; 30 minutes computer time.

Previous skills/knowledge needed

The children need to have collected data and to have entered it into a simple database in order to produce bar charts and pie charts – see 'Traffic jam' on page 64 and 'Shampoo and set' on page 67.

Key background information

Where the children have undertaken previous activities involving the collection of data, they may not (due to time constraints or the availability of equipment) have had the opportunity to fully demonstrate their ability to produce bar charts or pie diagrams. This activity focuses purely on this aspect of handling information, and is not set in any particular context.

Language to be introduced

Menu option, data file.

Preparation

Most information handling software contains sample data files, which are ideal for this activity. Make sure that some are easily accessible to the children, perhaps creating a special directory on the hard disk or a floppy disk. Check that they have not been modified from their original form. Make a list of the data files available.

Resources needed

A computer with a program which can produce bar charts and pie charts from lists of data, prepared data files suitable for the production of bar charts and pie charts, a list of the data files available.

What to do

Explain to the children that the main purpose of this activity is to enable you to see how far they have progressed in their ability to create graphs from data on screen. Demonstrate how to load an existing data file into the program, but do not remind them how to generate graphs. Tell them that the task is to choose from the list of data files in order to produce one bar chart and one pie chart. In each case, the type of graph created should be appropriate to the data.

Suggestion(s) for extension

Ask all the children to add comments to their finished graphs, and note the quality of these. In particular, ask the more able children to include some inferential comments in addition to straightforward ones – that is, to comment on the significance of the data as opposed to simply commenting on the numerical information.

Suggestion(s) for support

Some children may need the support of an adult or a more confident partner in order to load a data file from the disk.

Assessment opportunities

Assessment of data handling is the main focus of this activity. Through careful observation and discussion, you may be able to assign a 'best fit' in relation to the level descriptions for IT in Key Stage 1.

DISCOVERY

To be introduced to the use of a CD-ROM for information handling.

✝✝ *Whole-class discussion; activity in groups of 3.*

🕐 *30–45 minutes discussion/demonstration time; 30 minutes computer time.*

Previous skills/knowledge needed
The children should have developed confidence in generic IT skills, such as selecting with the mouse and pointer, recognising screen icons and using menus. They should be able to cope with the level of difficulty of the text in the particular CD-ROM being used for this activity.

Key background information
The CD-ROM has now become almost a standard classroom resource. There is an ever-increasing variety to choose from, including interactive and encyclopaedia CD-ROMs. The encyclopaedia type is an excellent classroom resource for reference work, and CDs are available to cover most areas of the curriculum. The ability to access a wide variety of information in textual, picture, sound or video format makes reference and research activities using CD-ROMs enjoyable and rewarding. Usually, the text and images can be selected and placed into word-processing or DTP software.

Different CD-ROMs have different ways of allowing you to access the information. The encyclopaedia type usually has an efficient search routine, and sometimes has a logical search facility. Typically, a *search routine* is accessed by entering the name of the item into a text box. For example, entering 'Romans' would produce a list of all references to this subject. A *logical search* allows two or more attributes to be sought for at the same time. For example, entering 'Romans' and 'Britain' would confine the references to Roman Britain (as opposed to the whole of Roman history). Other types of access may be of the 'browse around' kind, in which a search routine is not an integral feature.

Given the vast amount of information available, the children need to develop skills that allow them to search such IT systems efficiently. It is all too easy to browse around irrelevant areas of information within CD-ROMs, jumping hopefully from link to link or wandering off course. A systematic approach is needed which enables the children to develop appropriate skills and strategies.

Many of the CD-ROMs used widely at Key Stage 1 do not involve any IT skills except for generic ones, such as selecting with the mouse. However, the skills necessary for handling information are common to a variety of media. Whether you are using a book, a videotape, a photograph, a visit or a CD-ROM, the sequence of activities is generally as follows:

▲ Think about the information you want to find.

▲ Look for the information.

▲ Record what you find.

▲ Present the information.

Children's computer time is frequently limited. In order to make the most efficient use of a CD-ROM, they should have specific tasks to perform – and, if appropriate, be working within a set time-limit. The activity which follows prepares children for 'multi-tasking': using more than one application at a time, such as a word processor, a graphics program and a CD-ROM.

Language to be introduced
CD-ROM, search.

Preparation
As with any classroom resource, it is essential to have a good knowledge of the contents of the CD-ROM that you plan to use with the children. Search it to identify the kind of information that you would like the children to find out.

Prepare a number of question sheets (see 'What to do') which will help them to target specific areas of information. A typical context is finding out about 'minibeasts'. You could ask the children to find information on different minibeasts' habitat, type of movement, number of legs, whether they are insects or not, and so on. Photocopiable page 127 could be used as a basis for this by writing suitable questions on a copy of the sheet and making further copies of the resulting question sheet.

Resources needed

A computer with a CD-ROM drive, a printer (preferably in colour), an encyclopaedia CD-ROM, question sheets (see 'Preparation'), writing materials.

What to do

In the context of a specific theme (such as minibeasts), introduce a task which requires the children to find information from a variety of conventional sources such as library books, pictures, photographs, posters and videos. Introduce an appropriate CD-ROM, pointing out that it probably contains more information than all the other sources put together. Ask them how useful it would be for this particular task if they had a thousand books on minibeasts. Lead the discussion around to the idea that this vast amount of information would be of little immediate use if (a) you didn't know what specific information you wanted, and (b) you had to look at all the books to see what they contained.

Demonstrate how to put the CD-ROM into the computer's CD-ROM drive. Show the children how to find information on specific topics by choosing from the index or (if appropriate) by clicking on icons. Ask the children to suggest a few possible questions – for example, *Where do ants live?* Talk them through the process of finding this information.

Show them the question sheets you have prepared and ask them to add some questions of their own. As they find things out, they should write down the answers on another sheet of paper. Next, they should present the information found in their own way – perhaps writing two or three sentences or 'bullet points' per answer, with a sketch. Organise the class into groups of three and arrange a rota for them to use the computer, setting a time-limit for each group.

Suggestion(s) for extension

The question sheets can be tailored to individual children's specific abilities; where appropriate, they could demand a more thorough search for information. For example, more confident children could be asked to identify and name the parts of an insect's body.

Suggestion(s) for support

Similarly, the task could be simplified for less confident children by limiting the number of questions, and by providing suitable prompts for guidance on the question sheet.

Assessment opportunities

Note the techniques the children use for finding information. Look for evidence of a systematic and efficient approach, such as using the index rather than searching randomly.

Display ideas

The information that the children have recorded on their question sheets could be displayed alongside other work on the topic and any posters or pictures which were supplied with the CD-ROM. Appropriate pictures could be downloaded from the CD-ROM (see 'CD snaps' below) by the teacher and displayed with the children's work.

Previous skills/knowledge needed

The children should have used a CD-ROM to find information – see 'Discovery' on page 73. They should be able to copy and paste when using a word processor or graphics package.

Key background information

See 'Discovery' (page 73) for background information on CD-ROMs as information sources. With the advent of CD-ROMs, e-mail and the Internet, the technique of copying and pasting has become an essential IT skill for information handling. An emerging problem, however, is the

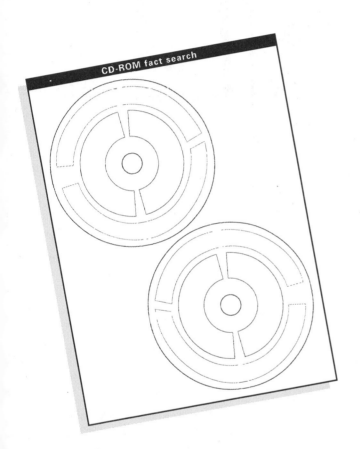

indiscriminate use of the facility. There is now so much information available from a range of electronic sources that it is almost impossible to trace the 'true' origin of any quote or picture. This has led to claims that some students and journalists simply pass off a collage of other people's material as their 'own' written work. This had always been a possibility when conventional sources were used; but the fact that electronic copying and pasting does not require any physical contact with the text makes plagiarism far easier both to carry out and to disguise.

Sometimes, in work with young children, the same problems can arise. Computer literacy is a popular alternative to literacy, and a child with appropriate IT skills can go a long way towards avoiding the task of composing and writing information text. Attractive presentations which include text and pictures do not necessarily represent an appropriate learning experience. The activity which follows involves children in finding information and undertaking DART (Directed Activities Related to the Text), in order to ensure that they engage with the text at the level of meaning as well as the level of its appearance or surface features.

One of the most useful features of modern IT programs is that they can often be used concurrently. As children write on the screen using a word processor, they can open a graphics package, draw a picture and import this into the

Reference to photocopiable sheet

Photocopiable page 127 is a blank question sheet with spaces for the topic title, and for the teacher's and children's questions.

CD SNAPS

To practise the use of a CD-ROM for information handling. To copy and paste from a CD-ROM to a word processor.

†† *Whole-class discussion; activity in groups of 3.*

🕐 *30 minutes discussion/activity time; 30–45 minutes computer time (2 sessions).*

INFORMATION TECHNOLOGY

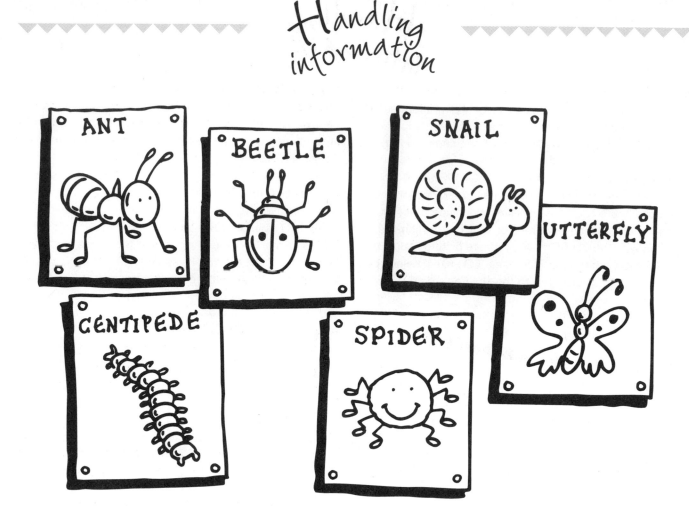

text. (See 'How it looks' on page 30.) Similarly, any text or picture in an encyclopaedia CD-ROM can be copied and pasted into another document.

The 'copy and paste' technique is very similar whichever system is being used. Usually, you start by highlighting the piece of text or picture on screen. You then select Edit and Copy. Most CD-ROMs also include the conventional icon for *copy* on the toolbar. Once the piece has been *copied*, it can be *pasted* into the document by placing the cursor at the appropriate point and selecting Edit and Paste (or clicking on the *paste* icon on the toolbar).

Language to be introduced
Copy, paste, toolbar.

Preparation
As with the 'Discovery' activity (page 73), it is essential for you to have a sound knowledge of what the CD-ROMs to be used contain. Never ask the children to use a CD-ROM that you have not looked at yourself. In particular, be careful when using material which is not specifically written for children. Try searching for information related to the current topic, so that you can suggest appropriate starting points and questions for the children to pursue.

Multi-tasking involves a lot of computer memory, so check that your equipment can cope with it. If necessary, restrict the amount of information that the children are allowed to copy and paste. Make one copy per child of the

question sheet used in the 'Discovery' activity (based on photocopiable sheet 127), and several copies per child of the 'CD snaps' ideas sheet (photocopiable page 128).

Resources needed
A computer with a CD-ROM drive, an encyclopaedia CD-ROM, a printer (preferably colour), question sheets (see 'Preparation'), photocopiable sheet 128.

What to do
In an appropriate curriculum context, refer to the children's previous experience of finding information from an encyclopaedia CD-ROM. (In the sample presentations on photocopiable page 128, the topic is 'Minibeasts'.) Remind them what they did with the information, perhaps illustrating this with some of their previous work. Now discuss the way in which text can be copied and pasted within a document, again using some of the children's previous work as an example. (See 'Wax lyrical' on page 36.)

Demonstrate how to put the CD-ROM into the computer's CD-ROM drive and find some relevant information on it. Ask the children whether they recognise any icons on the screen, drawing their attention in particular to the *copy* and *paste* icons. Invite suggestions about how this facility could be used, steering the discussion towards the idea of copying text from the CD-ROM to the word processor. Show them how this is done, talking through the process as you do so. Ask for volunteers to carry out the procedure until you are sure that all the children understand it. Next, choose a picture and repeat the *copy* and *paste* sequence with it.

Give the children the question sheets you have prepared and ask them to add their own questions. Explain that they will have to find the answers by copying and pasting from the CD-ROM onto the word processor, then selecting and arranging suitable material to create a printed information sheet:

▲ As they find out information, they should copy and paste relevant sections of text and any diagrams or pictures onto blank pages on the word processor. Restrict the amount of text and the number of pictures each group can collect, depending on the amount of computer memory and time available.

▲ Once they have stored the information in the word processor, the task is to look through it and select only the most useful pieces, then present the information in their own way. Draw their attention to photocopiable page xxx, which offers some suggestions for presentation. Suggest parameters for the finished product – for example, no more than ten lines of text and two diagrams or pictures. Emphasise that their presentation should not be a simple facsimile of the original. Direct excerpts (in a suitable arrangement) are acceptable, but they should also present some information in their own words.

Organise groups of three to take turns in using the computer, and set a time-limit for each group. It may be useful to organise two sessions, one for the initial copying into the word processor and another for working on the presentation. The second task does not require a CD-ROM system, so another computer could be used.

Suggestion(s) for extension
The question sheets could be tailored to individual children's specific abilities, and demand a more thorough search for information. More open-ended tasks could be set, such as 'Find out about animals with more than eight legs' rather than closed questions such as 'How many legs does a centipede have?'

Suggestion(s) for support
Similarly, the task could be simplified for less confident children by limiting the number of questions, and by providing suitable prompts for guidance on the question sheet.

Assessment opportunities
Look for confidence in cutting and pasting from one application to another. Note which children use the cut and paste technique again to refine their presentations.

Display ideas
The children's final products are an obvious source of display material. They could be printed out and mounted, or combined into a single document – with a title such as *Everything You Ever Wanted To Know About Minibeasts* – on the computer for people to browse through.

Reference to photocopiable sheet
Photocopiable page 128 provides some suggested layouts for the completed information. Children could attempt to replicate these, or create variants on them, when presenting their 'answer' pages.

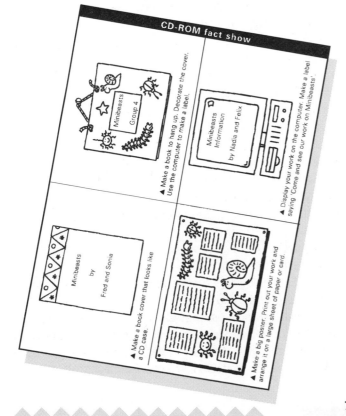

WEATHER WATCH

To practise making and collecting accurate observations. To enter the data into a simple spreadsheet.

♦♦ *Whole-class discussion; paired or small-group activity.*

🕐 *Discussion/data-collection time ongoing over a period of 1 or 2 weeks; short sessions of computer time during the activity period.*

Previous skills/knowledge needed
The children should have had experience of entering information about the weather onto a (paper) class weather chart. They should have recorded, from direct observation, aspects of the weather such as the amount of cloud and the strength and direction of the wind.

Language to be introduced
Spreadsheet, cell.

	temperature	rainfall	wind direction	wind force	sunshine	cloud
Monday	15	0	SW	4	DULL	VERY
Tuesday	16	0	W	3	MIXED	SOME
Wednesday	17	0	W	2	CLEAR	LITTLE
Thursday						
Friday						*Figure 3*

Key background information

A *spreadsheet* is simply a grid containing a number of rectangles or 'cells' arranged in rows and columns. However, there are major differences between a computer spreadsheet and an ordinary table or grid. Spreadsheets allow information to be sorted and presented automatically in a variety of ways. They also have more complex applications to do with modelling and prediction; these arise in IT work at Key Stage 2/Scottish Levels C–E, and are discussed in *Curriculum Bank Information Technology (Key Stage 2)*.

In this activity, an introductory spreadsheet is used to generate graphs in order to display weather records organised according to simple criteria. For example, the 'temperature' column of the spreadsheet shown in Figure 3 could be used directly to generate a graph (see Figure 4).

Preparation

Prepare a large blank weather grid (photocopiable page 129 could be enlarged for this purpose) on paper or card. Replicate the rows and columns in a simple spreadsheet and save this on disk.

Resources needed

A computer with a simple spreadsheet program, a colour printer, a large blank weather grid (see 'Preparation'), a spreadsheet replicating the weather grid, suitable instruments (such as measuring cylinders and thermometers) for making weather observations.

What to do

In the context of work on 'Weather', discuss the children's previous experiences of recording the weather. *Why were they doing this? Why is information about the weather useful? Who might need to use it?* Introduce the idea of using a table or grid to record the weather each day.

Enter imaginary data into the large weather grid, discussing and agreeing on ways to record different weather conditions. For example *What would be the best way to record the wind strength: on a scale of 1 to 10, or with adjectives such as weak, moderate and strong? How can rainfall be measured? How many adjectives should be allowed as options to record the degree of sunshine?*

Once the terminology and measures have been established, set up a rota for pairs or small

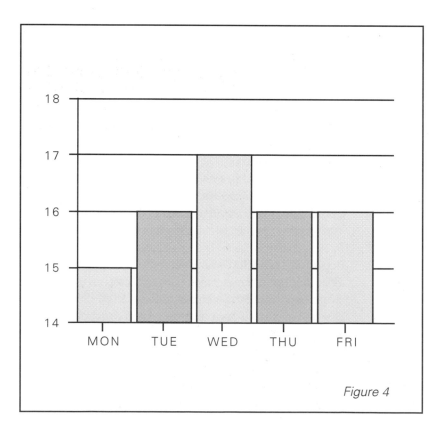
Figure 4

INFORMATION TECHNOLOGY

groups to record weather details on a daily basis. Provide equipment as appropriate. Ask them to enter their data onto the class grid.

Once the weather chart has been filled in for a few days, introduce the spreadsheet; ask the children to enter the information from the class grid into the appropriate cells. Now demonstrate how to create graphs from the columns. The exact method will depend on the particular software being used, but it normally involves highlighting the data and choosing a type of graph from a menu. Demonstrate how to choose a bar chart, pie diagram or line graph, and discuss the appropriateness of each. The line graph will only be appropriate for a 'continuous variable' such as temperature.

Set up a rota for the pairs or groups to take turns in producing graphs from the information.

Suggestion(s) for extension
If time allows, more confident children could be encouraged to enter information which they have gathered during previous activities. For example, data from the 'Traffic jam' activity (see page 65) could be entered. They could experiment with the software to produce different kinds of graphs.

Suggestion(s) for support
Less confident children are likely to need adult support at each stage of this activity. The text or numbers entered into the cells should be checked for accuracy and consistency. For example, the computer will regard 'a lot' and 'lots' as different values, so adjectives need to be written consistently.

Assessment opportunities
Note the extent to which the children can highlight cells and produce graphs independently.

Display ideas
The two types of weather grid – the large written version and the printed spreadsheet – could be displayed alongside

each other, together with the graphs the children have produced. Appropriate illustrations or graphics could be added.

Reference to photocopiable sheet
Photocopiable page 129 is a sample weather grid which could be enlarged for use as a wall chart in the activity.

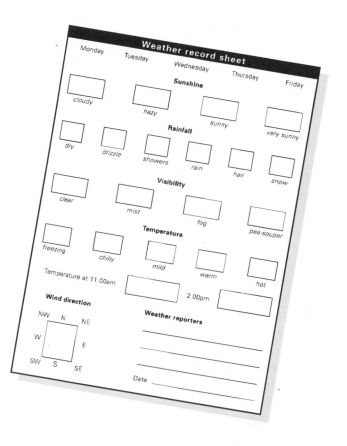

HOW DOES IT FEEL?

To practise making and collecting accurate observations. To enter this information into a simple spreadsheet. To sort the data using particular criteria.

†† *Whole class or groups.*

🕐 *30–45 minutes discussion/activity time.*

Previous skills/knowledge needed
The children should know what a spreadsheet is. They should have sufficient keyboard skills to enter 'yes' and 'no' into a cell within a spreadsheet, and to highlight groups of cells using the 'click and drag' technique with the mouse.

Key background information
'Weather watch' on page 77 provides some background information about spreadsheets. This activity which follows involves the sorting of data using specific criteria. For

INFORMATION TECHNOLOGY

	hard	soft	light	heavy	shiny	natural	manmade
Raw wool	no	yes	yes	no	no	yes	no
Pebble	yes	no	no	yes	yes	yes	no
Plastic cotton reel	yes	no	yes	no	yes	no	yes
Leather glove	no	yes	yes	no	yes	yes	no

Figure 5

example, children sorting materials according to their properties might come up with a list as follows:

Raw wool	soft	light	furry	natural
Pebble	hard	heavy	shiny	natural
Plastic cotton reel	hard	light	shiny	man-made
Leather glove	soft	light	shiny	natural/ man-made

This information could be entered into a spreadsheet in the way shown in Figure 5. It would then be easy to sort the data. For example, all the 'man-made' materials could be found by highlighting the 'man-made' column and sorting alphabetically. (See Figure 6.) The exact method will depend on the particular spreadsheet being used. It is essential that you become familiar with this process before attempting to sort data on screen with the children.

The advantage of using a spreadsheet for sorting becomes apparent when you consider very long lists of information. In this example, the greater the number of different materials listed, the more significant the speed of the spreadsheet becomes.

The Programmes of Study for IT do not specify particular data-handling activities. At Key Stage 1 or Scottish Levels A–B, children should be taught to enter information into an existing database. This activity extends their capability further, since they are involved in preparing the database with the teacher. However, activities that offer opportunities for children to extend their experience to Level 3 are perfectly justified (see the Introduction on page 5).

Preparation

Provide samples of a range of materials (about ten will suffice) for sorting. Prepare a spreadsheet (based on photocopiable page 130) which lists the materials to be sorted. Enter some – but not all – of the criteria which you plan to elicit from the children when discussing how they might describe the properties of the materials. Make one copy per child of photocopiable page 130. Practise sorting the information on screen (see 'What to do').

Resources needed

A computer with an introductory-level spreadsheet, a range of materials for sorting, writing materials, photocopiable page 130.

What to do

In the context of work on the properties of materials in science, set the children the task of sorting a variety of materials according to several criteria. Ask them to suggest appropriate criteria. Show or remind them how Venn diagrams can be used to record which set a particular item belongs to. Figure 7 shows an example.

When the children have drawn Venn diagrams to sort the materials according to a range of criteria, ask them to describe certain items in terms of their properties.

	hard	soft	light	heavy	shiny	natural	manmade
Raw wool	no	yes	yes	no	no	yes	no
Pebble	yes	no	no	yes	yes	yes	no
Leather glove	no	yes	yes	no	yes	yes	no
Plastic cotton reel	yes	no	yes	no	yes	no	yes

Figure 6

It is important here to agree about terminology. For example, just how shiny does an object have to be for the adjective 'shiny' to be appropriate as a description of it? How heavy is 'heavy'? – and so on.

Next, distribute the blank spreadsheets from photocopiable page 130 and help the children to complete the columns. they should start by listing the materials they have used. After entering the 'properties' as headings, they should complete the sheet by entering the agreed words or numbers in the cells. This may need to be done by groups working in turn, so that they all have the opportunity to handle the materials before recording their properties.

Next, introduce the spreadsheet you have prepared, drawing attention to the columns, rows and cells. Drawing on the children's suggestions, enter the items in the first column until you have listed all the materials that they have investigated. Point out the properties you have entered in the first row and ask them to suggest further ones, entering them into the spreadsheet as you go

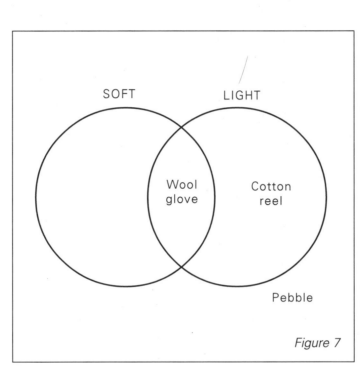

SOFT   LIGHT

Wool
glove

Cotton
reel

Pebble

Figure 7

along. When all the criteria have been entered, ask the children to help you fill in the cells by telling you which items are 'soft', 'heavy' and so on. Discuss how long it takes to look at the information and pick out those with certain properties. Demonstrate how to sort the complete information according to the required criteria. For example, to identify all the natural materials, highlight the whole sheet and 'sort' on the 'natural' column. This will group all the natural materials together. All the other cells will 'follow' the 'natural' cell, so that the information on all the properties of each item remains accurate. (Simply highlighting one column may misplace the information and render it inaccurate.) Try this out before showing the children. Discuss how quickly the computer carries out this operation, compared to the children's earlier work in recording the properties of different materials.

Let individual children take turns in sorting the information with your support. Ask them to think about who might find this facility useful. If possible,

INFORMATION TECHNOLOGY

arrange for groups of children to see a spreadsheet being used in the school office for listing children according to their age or the class they are in.

Suggestion(s) for extension

Some children may be able to enter data into a blank spreadsheet. For example, they could enter data previously collected – such as the hair and eye colour of children in the class – and add other information such as month of

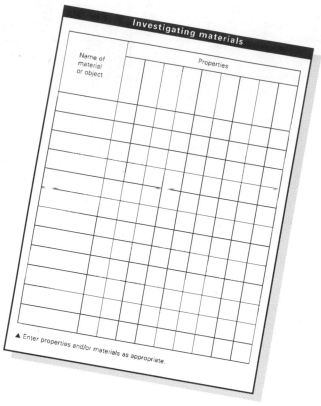

Investigating materials							
Name of material or object	Properties						

▲ Enter properties and/or materials as appropriate.

click

birth, favourite pop group and so on. They could then sort the data to find the most common hair colour or the most popular band.

Suggestion(s) for support

Care should be taken to involve less confident children in compiling the list of properties during the discussion. Entering 'yes' or 'no' into the appropriate cell should be within most children's capabilities, and will enable them to take an active part in the activity.

Display ideas

Versions of the spreadsheet with the materials sorted in different ways could be displayed on the wall alongside other work on materials and their properties. Signs could be added to the display, asking questions – such as *Are there more heavy objects than light objects?* or *Are all plastic objects bendy?* – which can be answered by reference to the displayed spreadsheets.

Reference to photocopiable sheet

Photocopiable page 130 is a blank table on which children can enter materials and their properties. It should be completed before you enter the information into the computer with the class.

The Spread Sheets

Modelling and control

The concept of computer modelling is often misunderstood as referring to visual representation. Computer modelling is mathematical in nature: it allows change in a real situation to be predicted, or a theory or idea to be tested and modified before being put into practice.

Many computer games provide opportunities for children to 'model' in various ways, presenting contexts for problem solving and leading to questions such as *'What would happen if?'*

The *My World* program offers opportunities for children to 'model' the real world using screen images; two activities related to this program are included here. However, modelling activities in this section relate chiefly to turtle geometry. Programming a floor robot or screen turtle is dependent on the ability to model or predict the path of the robot when it follows a series of simple commands.

This section also introduces children to control technology. Introductory activities dealing with switches and mechanical functions in everyday life lead into activities which involve using a simple programming language to give a sequence of commands. After some work on giving directional commands verbally, the floor robot is introduced. The commands used to move the robot are closely related to those used to move a screen turtle in the subsequent activities.

There is no agreed hierarchy for the development of skills in control; but the sequence of activities in this chapter reflects a progression from introductory work to tasks which are appropriate to Key Stage 2. They could also be used as in-service training activities for teachers who are unfamiliar with this area of IT.

INFORMATION
TECHNOLOGY

THE BEAR ESSENTIALS

To model a real-life process using modelling software. To develop keyboard skills.

†† *Whole-class discussion; paired activity.*

🕐 *15 minutes discussion/demonstration time; 15 minutes computer time.*

Key background information

Within the IT curriculum, the strand which appears to cause the most confusion among teachers is 'modelling'. (See the chapter introduction on page 83.) This activity and the next develop children's ability to use their computer skills in creating visual models of real-life situations.

screens for more complex activities can include several 'layers' of images.

Many of the *My World* screens provide opportunities to model real-life situations. This activity is suitable for very early work in IT, and takes its starting point from the everyday task of getting dressed.

Language to be introduced

Select, drag, drop.

Preparation

Dress a teddy bear with some clothes in the wrong order or position: gloves on feet, vest over shirt and so on. Load up the *My World* program ready to select the 'Teddy' screen (or a similar alternative).

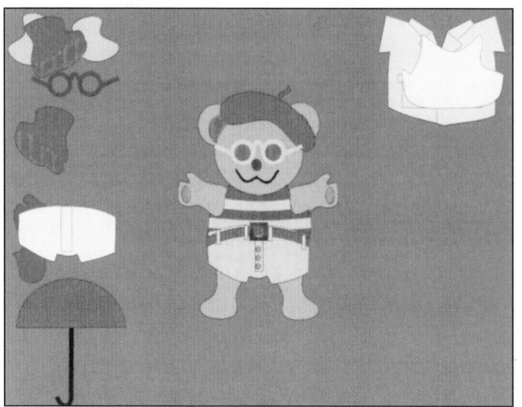

Figure 1a

The educational computer program *My World* (published by Inclusive Technology) presents children with pictures on a screen which they can move around by *dragging and dropping*. For example, a range of regular polygons including squares, rectangles and triangles can be moved to create a picture of a house or a rocket. Activities of this kind promote spatial awareness, as well as providing opportunities for children to develop keyboard skills.

Hundreds of different *My World* activities or 'screens' are available. All of these 'screens' are based on the same principle: parts of a picture (objects, shapes, numerals, human figures and so on) can be moved over a background. For example, furniture can be arranged within a kitchen. The screens for introductory activities are fairly simple; the

Resources needed

A computer with the program *My World* and a suitable screen such as 'Teddy', some teddy bears, a selection of dolls' clothes (which fit the teddy bears).

What to do

In the context of work on 'Ourselves' or another suitable topic (such as 'Weather'), discuss getting dressed.

Tell the children that your teddy bear has not quite learned how to get dressed; present the bear and ask them to say what is wrong. Discuss the order in which we put on clothes. Talk to them about how the seasons determine the clothes people wear, and ask them to suggest suitable (human) outfits for summer and winter.

INFORMATION TECHNOLOGY

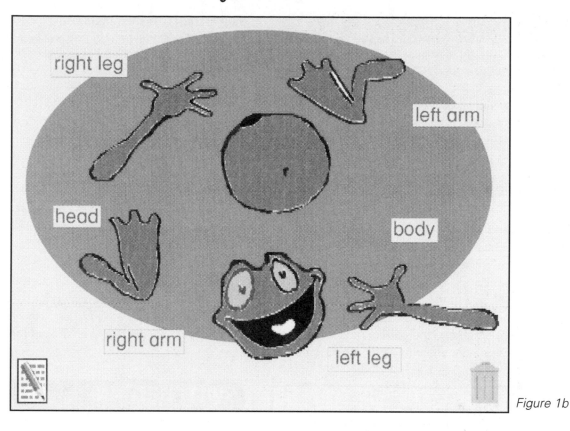

Figure 1b

Gather the children around the computer. Open up the 'Teddy' screen and demonstrate how an item of clothing can be moved around the screen by *dragging and dropping*. Show them how clothes can be placed on appropriate – and inappropriate – parts of the screen teddy bear, and also how they can be removed. Figure 1a shows the 'Teddy' screen being used in this way; Figure 1b shows a similar infant screen.

Organise pairings and devise a rota for each pair to have a turn at the computer. The task is to dress the teddy, choosing suitable clothes for either winter or summer. (If a child points out that bears hibernate in winter, suggest that the bear has woken up hungry and gone out for a snack.)

Suggestion(s) for extension
More confident children could be introduced to the text icon. When this is selected, a title can be given to the completed picture by typing letters into a box and pressing the *enter* key when the title is complete. The title can then be positioned on the screen using the *drop and drag* technique.

Suggestion(s) for support
Some children may need support in placing the items of clothes accurately on the bear. Although the program responds to a near miss by fitting the item in exactly the right position, accuracy requires good mouse control. Sometimes children find it useful to use both hands on the mouse in the early stages.

Assessment opportunities
Note those children who can place the clothes accurately, indicating good mouse control.

Display ideas
The completed screens could be printed out and used as part of an interactive display which invites children to dress an actual teddy bear (according to seasonal variations) using dolls' clothes. (Children's clothes can be used if the teddy bear is large enough.)

THAT'S LIFE!

To model a real-life process using a computer program. To develop keyboard skills further. To practise printing out work.

†† *Whole-class discussion; paired activity.*

🕐 *10 minutes discussion/demonstration time; 15 minutes computer time.*

Key background information
See 'The bear essentials' on page 84. Some *My World* screens provide pictures of a life cycle (for example, that of a butterfly or a frog) which are out of sequence.

Language to be introduced
Life cycle, sequence, print.

Preparation
Load up the *My World* program ready to select an appropriate screen (featuring an animal life cycle).

Resources needed
A computer with the program *My World* and a suitable screen.

What to do
In the context of work on 'Life cycles', introduce the screen to the children. Remind them how to move the pictures around, and ask them to suggest which of the pictures should be first and last. Ask for volunteers to move the pictures to the appropriate places, and invite comments. Work through the whole sequence in this way. Show the children how to print the completed life cycle, including how to choose the size of the print (if appropriate).

Arrange pairings and set the task: to produce a life cycle picture with the elements in the correct order on screen, and to print it out as independently as possible.

Suggestion(s) for extension
More confident children could be asked to write captions under each part of the life cycle, using the text facility.

Suggestion(s) for support
Ask less confident children to show you their completed screen before printing it out. Supervise the printing-out if necessary, trying to make sure that the children perform the operation themselves.

Assessment opportunities
Look for children placing the pictures with accuracy, indicating fine mouse control.

Display ideas
The completed life cycle printouts could be displayed with other work on this topic. Some printouts could be made with elements deliberately placed in the wrong sequence, with a caption inviting children to spot the mistakes.

SWITCHED ON

To know that switches control everyday devices.
†† *Whole class.*
🕐 *30–45 minutes.*
⚠ *The potential danger of electrical switches must be emphasised (see below).*

Previous skills/knowledge needed
No specific skills are required for this activity except general speaking and listening, and simple recording using a prepared sheet.

Key background information
A requirement of the National Curriculum for IT is that children should develop an awareness of the use of information and communication technology in everyday life. In relation to control technology, this means they should know that all electric and electronic devices have some kind of switch. This activity and the three which follow are designed to develop children's concepts of switching – from the simple external on/off switch to more complex switches which are often hidden from view. This activity could be combined with 'Turn it up' (page 88), which focuses on calibrated switches.

Language to be introduced
Switch, on/off.

Preparation
Bring into school a few familiar devices which have on/off switches, such as a torch, an alarm clock and a mobile

click

phone. Make one copy per child of photocopiable page 131.

Resources needed
Some familiar devices with on/off switches, photocopiable sheet 131, writing materials.

What to do
In the context of work on 'Science in everyday life' or 'Electricity', introduce the idea of switches. *What do they do? Why do we need them? What would happen if a particular machine (such as a kettle) could be switched on but not off?* Demonstrate how the switches work on a few familiar devices (see 'Resources needed').

Ask the children to look for switches around the classroom: the switches for the lights, the heater (if appropriate), the cassette player and so on. Set them the task of finding as many switches as possible around the school and at home. Explain that they should record their findings on a sheet of paper, under such headings as 'Living room', 'Kitchen' and 'Classroom'.

When the children have had time to complete this activity, discuss their findings, drawing out any general features. Do all the devices need electricity to work? Have the children found any unusual switches (such as a string to be pulled for light or shower heat)? Are some switches illuminated (such as those on a video recorder)? Has anyone identified the computer mouse as a switch?

⚠ Emphasise the importance of the children simply looking for switches, rather than using them or playing with them. Tell them that they must inform a parent or carer before searching for switches at home.

To finish the activity, give out copies of photocopiable sheet 131 and ask the children to identify the switches.

Suggestion(s) for extension
More confident children could be asked to think of switches they encounter outdoors, such as buttons at pelican crossings or the 'remote control' switches on automatic doors. They could also go on to 'Turn it up' (page 88) as an extension.

Suggestion(s) for support
Children who find recording difficult could be provided with suitable pages from catalogues, from which they could cut out pictures of relevant appliances; they could stick these pictures onto a sheet of paper.

Assessment opportunities
The children's completed lists and their circles on photocopiable sheet 131 will indicate how well they understand what a switch is.

Display ideas
The children's completed lists and one or two photocopiable sheets could be made into a book to be displayed with current science work.

Reference to photocopiable sheet
Photocopiable page 131 contains two pictures of rooms, on which children can mark the devices which have switches.

Find the switches

▲ Can you spot the switches? Put a red circle around each one.

▲ Put a blue circle around each switch you spotted at home.

INFORMATION TECHNOLOGY

TURN IT UP

To know that switches are often calibrated. To know that '1' usually signifies low and '10' usually signifies high.

👥 *Whole class.*

🕐 *30–45 minutes.*

⚠ *The potential danger of electrical switches must be emphasised (see below).*

Previous skills/knowledge needed
The children should have a basic understanding of the function of on/off switches.

Key background information
See 'Switched on' on page 86.

Language to be introduced
High, low, more, less, control.

Preparation
Bring into school a few devices which have calibrated switches, such as a portable cassette player, an iron and a food mixer. Make one copy for each child of photocopiable page 132.

Resources needed
A selection of devices with calibrated switches, photocopiable page 132.

What to do
In the context of work on 'Science in everyday life' or 'Electricity', discuss the children's previous experience and understanding of switches. Ask them whether they have noticed anything different about some switches: *Do they turn or move steadily instead of being flipped? Do they have notches, markings, letters or numbers?* Discuss the effect of moving or turning such switches in either direction.

What types of appliances need this kind of control? Demonstrate the effect of the volume switch on a radio, cassette player or television set.

Set the children the task of finding calibrated switches around the school or at home. Distribute the photocopiable sheet and explain that they should use it to record their findings by drawing the different kinds of calibrated switch. If they can find an example of either of the two switches drawn at the top of the sheet, they should write down where it appears.

When the children have completed the activity, discuss their findings. Are there any unusual switches? What do the numbers on the switch inside a refrigerator mean: is 5 a higher temperature than 1? Are all calibrated switches circular? How do you control the volume on a television set? What do **<** and **>** mean on a remote control?

⚠ Emphasise the importance of the children simply looking for switches, rather than using them or playing with them. Tell them that they must inform a parent or carer before searching for switches at home. Suggest that, if possible, they should ask an adult to demonstrate the effect of turning the switches in either direction.

Suggestion(s) for extension
More confident children could be asked to describe and draw imaginary control devices. For example, they might imagine switches which increase or reduce the power of the senses, resulting in telescopic eyes, ears that can hear through walls or skin that is not sensitive to pain.

Suggestion(s) for support

Children who find recording difficult could be provided with suitable pages from catalogues, from which they could cut out pictures of relevant appliances and stick them onto the photocopiable sheet.

Assessment opportunities

The children's completed photocopiable sheets will provide evidence of their understanding.

Display ideas

The children's completed photocopiable sheets could be made into a book to be displayed with current science work.

Reference to photocopiable sheet

Photocopiable page 132 is a pro-forma record sheet on which the children can draw and name the devices they find which have calibrated switches.

IN THE PICTURE

To know that computer icons are often used to represent functions.

†† *Whole class.*

🕐 *30 minutes.*

⚠ *Although this activity does not involve the children investigating real switches, they should be reminded that they should not interfere with any electrical equipment around the school or home.*

Previous skills/knowledge needed

The children should have a basic understanding of the function of switches.

Key background information

See 'Switched on' (page 86 for general information about switches in IT at this level.

The word *icon* in this context is used to describe any visual symbol which conveys a meaning. The idea of using icons (particularly ones with a religious significance) is traditional in the visual arts. Flags, badges and banners often make use of icons. They can be interpreted by speakers of most languages, and may be common to many countries. Using icons can save numerous words.

In relation to IT, icons on the computer screen are frequently used as a way of moving to various parts of a program or of performing a task. In this sense, the icon represents a *function* or particular job. For example, you can move a section of text as follows:

1. Highlight the text to be moved.
2. Click the mouse on a small picture of a pair of scissors (the 'cut' icon) to remove the section.
3. Move the cursor to the position where you wish the text to be placed, then click on the small picture of a paste brush (the 'paste' icon). The text will appear in the new position.

The icons used within different word-processing and other programs are usually very similar. This means that the skills and techniques developed when using one computer system can easily be transferred to another one.

INFORMATION TECHNOLOGY

Language to be introduced
Icon, remote control, sign.

Preparation
Bring into school a few devices that use icons to represent functions, such as a steam iron, a food mixer and a TV/video remote control unit. Make one copy per child of photocopiable page 133.

Resources needed
Some electrical devices that use icons to represent functions, photocopiable page 133.

What to do
In the context of work on 'Science in everyday life' or 'Electricity', introduce the idea of small pictures being used to represent something. Draw on the children's own experience of road traffic signs, 'no smoking' signs and so on. Introduce the word 'icon' and discuss the usefulness of icons in communication.

Point out the icons on the appliances you have brought in. Note (if appropriate) the picture of steam representing the 'steam' function on the iron, and the picture of a speaker with a cross through it depicting 'mute' on the TV remote control unit.

Ask the children to think of possible icons that could be used to represent everyday activities or instructions in the school – for example, 'wet playtime' or 'where the PE benches are stored'. If they could control many different things with a hand-held remote unit (such as lights, curtains or doors), what icons would they use for these things? Distribute copies of photocopiable page 133 and ask the children to fill in the buttons on the remote control unit, inventing suitable icons for each of the functions they would like to control.

Suggestion(s) for extension
More able children could be set the challenge of identifying some icons that are used across the world. Pictures in books about other countries might be a useful source of evidence, and children could ask their parents, relatives, carers and teachers whether they have seen traffic signs, airport signs, bus stops and so on during their trips abroad.

Suggestion(s) for support
Some children may need prompts to start them off on the task. Suggest some day-to-day functions such as opening and closing windows, and ask the children to suggest suitable icons for *open* and *close*. Encourage them to think of imaginary uses of a remote control unit, such as putting milk on cereal or combing hair, and to draw appropriate icons for these on the blank unit (photocopiable page 133).

Assessment opportunities
The children's completed pictures of a remote control unit (photocopiable page 133) will show how well they understand that the icon needs to give a clear indication of the associated function.

Display ideas
The completed 'remote control unit' pictures could be displayed underneath a suitable caption, such as 'Signs of the Times'.

Reference to photocopiable sheet
Photocopiable page 133 shows a blank remote control unit, which the children can complete by drawing icons on the buttons.

SECRET SWITCHES

To know that switches can be hidden and can respond to movement or to changes in pressure, light or temperature.

†† *Whole class.*

🕓 *Time for preparation, visit and follow-up as appropriate.*

⚠ *Children should be carefully supervised during the visit.*

Previous skills/knowledge needed
The children should have a basic understanding of the function of a switch. They should have investigated the use of switches in everyday life, including ones which are calibrated and ones which incorporate icons.

Key background information
See 'Switched on' (page 86).

Language to be introduced
Supermarket, sensor, bar code, Delta and Switch cards (bank cards used to pay funds directly from an account), thermostat, automatic.

Preparation
Thorough preparation is essential for this activity. Arrange for the class to visit a local supermarket (preferably one with which most of the children are familiar). Discuss the objectives of the visit with the supermarket manager beforehand. Make sure he/she knows the age of the children, as most stores will not allow young children to visit the non-public areas such as food preparation facilities. Arrange adult support for the visit.

Visit the store and prepare a suitable sequence for the class visit, noting all the possible uses of switches from the initial entry through to the final payment at the checkout. These are likely to include:

▲ illuminated signs which are timed to light up when the shop is open;

▲ 'automatic' doors which respond to signals from light-sensitive switches;

▲ switches for the overhead lights;

▲ freezers with a thermostatic switch to adjust the temperature;

▲ alarmed barriers which prevent people leaving by other routes than through the checkouts;

▲ switches to start and stop the conveyor belts at the checkouts;

▲ bar-code readers which are light-sensitive and respond to the black and white lines of a bar-code, translating this into a particular item and price at the checkout (and feeding the information back to automatic stock control systems);

▲ weighing machines (sometimes built into the surface of the checkout counter);

▲ card readers which are sensitive to the magnetic strip on a delta/switch card or bank card;

▲ cash machines, which often have icons to help the operator.

Obtain some pictures of supermarket scenes (for example, from a supermarket catalogue) for discussion. Make one copy per child of photocopiable page 134.

Resources needed
Adult support for the visit, pictures of a supermarket, a board or large sheet of paper, photocopiable page 134.

What to do
This activity can be focused specifically on IT, with all the children involved in finding information about switching and control; or it could be more broad-based, with only a group of the children looking at IT aspects. The visit should follow sufficient experience and discussion about the use of switches to control various devices.

Discuss the idea of 'automatic' switches, drawing out the idea that all switches need to be controlled in some way. For example, if the school has a secure entry system, show the children how doors are opened by remote control or by entering a code into a number pad. Some children may have a security system at home. Show the children some pictures of a supermarket and ask them to suggest where switches might be located, summarising their suggestions on the board or a large sheet of paper.

Tell the children about the proposed visit, making clear what they will be looking for and what you hope they will learn from the visit. Just before the visit, give out copies of

photocopiable page 134; explain that they will be using this sheet to record their findings.

Following the visit, initiate a discussion, perhaps by asking the children in turn (individually or in groups) to recall the details of their journey through the store. Ask them to say which switches they saw in each part of the store (if necessary, they can refer to their photocopiable sheets). Make sure that the discussion – for example, of the function of a thermostat or a bar-code reader – is matched to the children's level of understanding and experience.

Individuals or groups could contribute to a class book with drawings and captions featuring all of the control devices, switches, sensors and so on that they have found.

Suggestion(s) for extension
Children with a good understanding of the idea of switches being operated by sensors could draw designs for a high-security classroom.

Suggestion(s) for support
Careful grouping can ensure that the less confident children work with the more confident during the visit. Alternatively, a small group of children could be given focused support by an adult.

Assessment opportunities
A good impression of how well the children understand the use of control in everyday life could be gained from looking at the completed photocopiable sheets.

Display ideas
The completed class book about the visit could be displayed in the class (or school) library, or together with other work

on control technology. The children's designs for a high-security classroom (see 'Suggestion(s) for extension') could be displayed with a title such as *Lesson Impossible*.

Reference to photocopiable sheet
Photocopiable page 134 is a pro-forma record sheet which the children can use to record information about switches during their visit.

DIRECT A FRIEND

To understand the concept of moving forward or back and turning left or right in relation to a given position. To know that, in basic control technology activities, right/left 1 *indicates a turn of one right angle.*

†† *Whole class and pairs.*
🕐 *20–30 minutes.*

Key background information
The activities which follow this one introduce children to simple control technology devices such as floor robots and screen turtles. However, if young children are introduced to a floor robot without previous experience of work on directions, they often become confused and progress is hindered. Thus some initial work on establishing the concepts of *forward*, *backwards*, *left* and *right* (in relation

to a given position) will save time in the long run.

For example, confusion will sometimes arise when children direct a floor robot to move forward 1 unit, then turn 90° to the right, then move forward 1 more unit. If the robot were initially travelling 'forward' towards the front of the class, then when it is directed to move *forward 1* after the turn, children often expect it to continue towards the front of the class rather than towards the right-hand wall. They need to understand that changing the robot's orientation (which way it is facing) changes the direction of 'forward' relative to a wider frame of reference.

Because young children will not usually understand that degrees can be used as measures of turn, most floor robots allow a 90° turn to be entered as 1. Thus the command *right 2* would produce a turn of 180°.

Language to be introduced
Forward, back, backwards, right, left, pace, command.

Resources needed
A large space, sufficient for all the children to move about in freely.

What to do
Gather the class together in a large space. Tell the children that you want them to follow your exact directions. Establish what one *pace* and one *turn* (90°) mean. Ask them to follow a sequence such as: *Everyone face the window wall. Take*

one pace forward, take one pace back. Turn right 1. Take one pace forward…

Next, discuss shortened forms of these instructions, such as *forward 1* and *right 1*. Direct another sequence of movements using these abbreviations.

Organise the children into pairs and ask them to take turns directing each other. Restrict the maximum number of paces to three (to avoid major traffic jams) and the maximum number of turns to 4 (to avoid confusion and dizziness).

This activity usually leads to some confusion at first. Some children will not be sure of left and right, and many are likely to think that *forward* remains constant, resulting in some interesting chasse-type (sideways) movements. This, of course, is the whole point of the exercise, as the children will learn from their mistakes. The aim is to reach a common understanding about the instructions or commands.

Suggestion(s) for extension
More confident children could try to direct their partners through more complex paths, such as a figure of eight.

Suggestion(s) for support
Some children may need extra help in learning *right* and *left*. The support of an adult would be useful, and additional time might be needed. Suggest that the children practise in the playground, and encourage them to demonstrate to you when they think they have achieved success.

INFORMATION TECHNOLOGY

Assessment opportunities

Look for clear understanding of the difference between *forward/back* and *turn* commands, and for the ability to give *turn* commands without confusing left and right.

DIRECT A TOY

To develop the concept of moving forward or back and turning left or right in relation to a given position. To record commands using arrow symbols.

†† *Whole class and pairs.*

🕐 *30–45 minutes.*

Previous skills/knowledge needed

The children should have undertaken the activity 'Direct a friend' (see page 92). They should be developing an understanding of *forward*, *back*, *right* and *left* in relation to a given position.

turtles; photocopiable page 135 also has sample cards and blanks. The cards should be reasonably robust.

Resources needed

Cards with arrow symbols and numbers (see 'Preparation'), a selection of toys with a recognisable 'front' and 'back'.

What to do

Remind the children how they directed each other during the 'Direct a friend' activity (see page 92), using short commands such as *forward 1*. Introduce the idea of directing a toy. Organise the children into pairs and give them some time to work together: one giving commands, the other moving a toy. Ask the children to decide on an appropriate unit of movement (for example, the toy's length would probably be suitable).

Call the class back together and record a typical sequence of commands on the board. Ask them to suggest ways in which these commands might be recorded without writing them out in full. Direct the discussion until you have established that arrows could be used; then write the

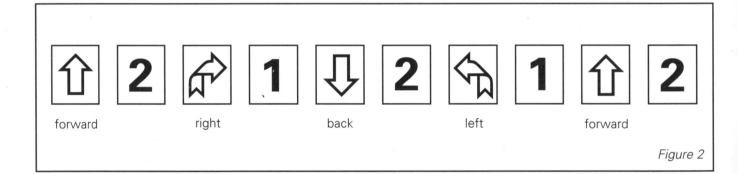

| forward | | right | | back | | left | | forward | |

Figure 2

Key background information

See 'Direct a Friend' on page 92. The most commonly available floor robots use arrow symbols for *forward*, *back*, *left* and *right*. This activity uses these symbols to introduce the idea of recording a sequence of commands – a *program* – which can be carried out by someone else.

Language to be introduced

Forward arrow, back arrow, left arrow, right arrow, program.

Preparation

Obtain a selection of toys such as cars, animals or model dinosaurs. The toys used must have a recognisable 'front' and 'back'.

Prepare cards (one set per pair of children) with the written command and arrow symbols for *forward*, *back*, *left* and *right*, and with the numbers 1, 2, 3 and 4. The arrow cards should exactly replicate the symbols on the floor robot which will be used in subsequent activities. Pre-printed cards are available from some suppliers of floor

original sequence using arrow symbols.

Introduce to the class the arrow and number cards, and show how they can be laid out in order to record a logical sequence of commands. An example is shown in Figure 2. Talk through several such examples then distribute the cards among the pairs of children and ask them to record a sequence of commands for their toys. Once everyone has completed this task, move one person from each pair to someone else's toy. Each child can then proceed through the sequence on the cards, moving the toy accordingly.

Introduce the idea that such a sequence of symbolic commands can be written down and saved for future use. Use the word *program* and write this word on the board. Point out that the spelling of *program* is different from that of *programme*, a word which they may have come across in relation to TV and radio.

Suggestion(s) for extension

The concepts developed in this activity are more fully developed in 'Robot walk' (page 96). More confident

INFORMATION TECHNOLOGY

children could be asked to suggest and record a sequence of commands which would end with the toy returning to its original position. This could be undertaken either with cards or on paper.

Suggestion(s) for support
Less confident children may need additional time to understand the relationship between the arrow symbols and the actual movement of the toy. The pairs could be organised so that less confident children have the support of more confident classmates.

Assessment opportunities
Note how well the children demonstrate an understanding of the relationship between the sequence of arrow symbols and the actual movement of the toy. Note whether they use the appropriate vocabulary to express their commands in succinct form – for example, saying 'forward 1' rather than 'that way a little bit'.

Display ideas
The various sequences of commands could be displayed alongside a map of the toys' movements across the floor. Co-ordinated toy movement sequences could be written to spell out messages.

Reference to photocopiable sheet
Photocopiable page 135 can be duplicated onto card and cut up to provide arrow, number and blank cards as required.

ROBOT WALK

To reinforce the concept of moving forward or back and turning left or right in relation to a given position. To practise recording commands using arrow symbols. To be introduced to programming a floor robot using a sequence of commands.

†† *Whole class and groups of 3 or 4.*

🕐 *30–40 minutes.*

⚠ *Make sure that floor robots are not used on tables.*

Previous skills/knowledge needed

The children should have undertaken suitable introductory activities, such as 'Direct a friend' (page 92) and 'Direct a toy' (page 94). They should have a good understanding of *forward*, *back*, *right* and *left* in relation to a given position, and be able to devise a sequence of commands using arrow symbols.

Key background information

Floor and table robots provide an ideal introduction to control

technology. The way that they are programmed is a simpler model of more sophisticated and complex programming used by professionals. A simple language or *syntax* is used to communicate a sequence of instructions or commands. A specific set of commands is called a *procedure*. Particular sequences can be repeated and procedures built up and saved for future use.

The use of a floor robot also develops and reinforces geometrical concepts. It can be programmed to turn through various angles in either a right or a left direction; many control activities at Key Stage 1 involve making the robot trace out regular polygons, such as a square or a hexagon. Work with a floor robot leads directly on to work with 'turtle geometry' or 'Logo' on the computer. The syntax used is very similar. Control activities at Key Stage 2, which involve the use of sensors to monitor changes in temperature, light, sound and so on, are dependent on a good knowledge of this kind of simple programming.

Activities with floor robots should not be undertaken on a table top, as they are likely to fall over the edge and be damaged. It is easy for both experienced and inexperienced operators to enter *forward 11* rather than *forward 1*, resulting in more movement than was intended! Carpeted floors can be used if the pile is not too deep, but this will sometimes result in slight inaccuracies. Some smaller versions of programmable robots are designed for use by younger children, and can safely be used on a table top.

Examples of floor robots are the Roamer (Valiant Technology) and the Pip (Swallow Systems). The Pixie (Swallow Systems) is designed for use on a table-top or floor. (N.B. To move the Pixie forward a specific number of units, instead of entering a number, it is necessary to press the *forward* arrow that number of times.) It is important to read the manual for the particular robot being used, since (although they are all very similar) some of the abbreviations and symbols recognised by the robot may be slightly different from those given in the activities in this chapter.

Language to be introduced
Forward arrow, back arrow, left arrow, right arrow, program, sequence, procedure.

Preparation
Prepare a programmable robot, such as the Valiant Roamer, by configuring it to turn through 90° when *right 1* or *left 1* is entered. Some robots have a built-in sequence which operates the first time that *Go* is pressed. Cancel this from the robot's memory before starting the activity.

Prepare cards with arrow symbols and numbers (see 'Direct a toy' on page 94), plus a 'Go' card. Photocopiable pages 135 and 136 can be duplicated onto card for this purpose. Make one copy per child of the 'Roamer keyboard' sheet (photocopiable page 137), or draw a similar one appropriate to the robot being used.

Resources needed
A programmable floor or table robot, arrow and number cards, 'Go' cards, photocopiable page 136 (or a similar sheet appropriate to the robot being used). A smooth, flat floor surface will be necessary for this and subsequent floor robot activities.

What to do
Gather the children around the robot on the floor, and ask them to point out its features. Does it have a front and back? Does it have a control panel? Ask them whether they recognise any numbers or symbols that they have used previously when 'programming' their friends or their toys. Ask for volunteers to make the robot go forwards, go backwards, turn left and turn right using the control keys. Discuss which keys they have pressed, and draw attention to the similarity of these commands to those which the children have used in previous activities.

Drawing on the children's suggestions, build up a few movement sequences. Tell the children that the robot automatically saves the last sequence of commands until it is programmed to do something else. Demonstrate this by pressing the 'Go' key several times. Show them how to cancel a sequence and start again.

Remind the children of the arrow and number cards that they have used previously. Give out the cards and ask volunteers to place them in the right sequence as each command is entered. Is there a card missing? Introduce the 'Go' card, and ask the children to place this at the end of each sequence.

Organise the children into groups of three or four and devise a rota for them to try programming the robot independently. If they are using the Roamer, distribute copies of photocopiable page 137 and ask the children to complete the labelling.

Suggestion(s) for extension
The following activities can be used to extend the children's experience of programmable robots: 'Slalom' (page 98) and 'Obstacle course' (page 99).

INFORMATION TECHNOLOGY

Command and bracket cards

Go [ ] [ ]

R W P

Procedure

The Roamer keyboard

▲ Write in the missing labels on this picture of a Roamer keyboard.

Forward

Cancel memory

Number keys

SLALOM

To practise programming a floor or table robot.

†† *Whole class and groups of 3 or 4.*

🕐 *15–20 minutes.*

Previous skills/knowledge needed

The children should have some experience of entering commands into a floor robot and recording sequences with arrow and number cards.

Key background information

See 'Robot walk' on page 96.

Preparation

Prepare arrow, number and 'Go' cards (photocopiable pages 135 and 136 can be duplicated onto card for this purpose). Set up three skittles in a line, about 60cm apart.

Resources needed

A programmable floor or table robot, three skittles or other markers; arrow, number and 'Go' cards (see 'Preparation').

What to do

Remind the children of their previous experience of programming the robot and using cards to record a sequence of commands. Gather all the children around the line of skittles and walk through the skittles, using the 'slalom' route you want the robot to follow. Ask one or two children to walk through the same route.

Set the task, which is to program the robot so that it will negotiate the slalom route without touching any skittles. The children should record their sequence of commands

Suggestion(s) for support

Make sure that less confident children work with others who are more confident. If possible, provide additional time and adult support for any children who experience difficulty in carrying out the tasks.

Assessment opportunities

Note how accurately the children enter commands, and their level of confidence in handling the robot.

Reference to photocopiable sheets

Photocopiable page 135 can be duplicated onto card and cut up to provide arrow, number and blank cards as required. Photocopiable page 136 can be used in the same way to provide 'Go' cards for this activity. Photocopiable page 137 is a diagram of a Roamer keyboard; if the children are using a Roamer in this activity, they can be asked to label the diagram.

INFORMATION TECHNOLOGY

using the cards. Organise working groups of about three or four and devise a rota for them to take turns carrying out the task.

Suggestion(s) for extension
Some children could try to program the robot to return to its original starting position.

Suggestion(s) for support
Try to make sure that less confident children work with more confident ones; if possible, provide adult support.

Assessment opportunities
Note how frequently children make mistakes. Look for those who adopt a systematic approach rather than relying on trial and error.

Display ideas
The children could draw a plan of the route around the skittles and display it alongside the sequence of commands. This could be elaborated into a picture of a floor robot on a ski slope.

Reference to photocopiable sheets
Photocopiable pages 135 and 136 have sample command cards, which can be duplicated for this activity.

OBSTACLE COURSE

To practise more flexible programming of a floor robot.
†† *Whole class and groups of 3 or 4.*
🕐 *15–20 minutes.*

Previous skills/knowledge needed
The children should have some experience of entering commands into a floor robot and recording sequences with arrow and number cards.

Key background information
See 'Robot walk' on page 96.

Preparation
Set up an obstacle course on the classroom floor, using between two and four obstacles and varying the distance between them from 40cm to 60cm. Make sure there is an adequate supply of command cards.

Resources needed
A programmable floor robot; arrow, number and 'Go' cards (see photocopiable pages 135 and 136); a few skittles, boxes, books and so on to provide obstacles.

What to do
Remind the children of their previous experience of programming the floor robot. Gather all the children around the obstacle course and walk though it several times, using a variety of routes. Ask one or two children to walk through the course, negotiating the obstacles. Discuss the distances involved in relation to the robot's unit of movement. For example, Roamer uses its own length (about 30cm) as a standard unit. Most robots can be configured to move in units of 1cm or more.

To set the context for this task, reference could be made to the Wallace and Gromit animation *The Wrong Trousers*, in which a burglary is carried out by a robot (a mechanical pair of trousers) under the control of a disguised penguin (who is using a remote control box). Organise working groups of about three or four and devise a rota for them to carry out the task, which is as follows:
▲ One or two children plan and set out an obstacle course on the floor.
▲ The rest of the group program the robot to negotiate the course.
▲ The children should record the successful sequence of commands using the cards.

Suggestion(s) for extension
Some children could try to arrange the whole sequence of cards in advance, rather than using them to record each move as they go along.

Suggestion(s) for support
Try to make sure that less confident children work with more confident ones; if possible, provide adult support.

INFORMATION TECHNOLOGY

Assessment opportunities

Note how accurately the children program the robot to negotiate the obstacle course, and whether they learn quickly through trial and improvement.

Display ideas

The children could draw a plan of the route around the course and display it alongside the sequence of commands. This could be elaborated into an imaginative context: using the robot to negotiate dangerous territory or to get through a security system.

Reference to photocopiable sheets

Photocopiable pages 135 and 136 have sample command cards, which can be duplicated for this activity.

ROBOPOSTMAN

To practise programming a floor or table robot. To use the 'Wait' command.

†† *Whole class, then groups of 3 or 4.*

🕐 *30 minutes discussion/demonstration time; 15–20 minutes activity time (per group).*

Previous skills/knowledge needed

The children should have some experience of entering commands into a floor robot and recording sequences with arrow and number cards.

Key background information

See 'Robot walk' on page 96. Some floor robots include a 'Wait' command. This needs to be followed by a number, indicating the number of seconds the robot should wait before carrying out the next command in the sequence. (It would not be accurate to say that the robot is inactive during this time, since in later work with sensors the robot might be programmed to wait specifically for a change in sound, light or temperature – a state which corresponds to 'active' waiting in a person.)

This activity can be enhanced by making the robot look like a postman with a cap and a bag containing letters. The use of the robot can then be more interactive, with children taking letters from the bag when the robot stops at each 'delivery' point.

The Roamer also has a music key which allows a range of notes to be played. The key press needs to be followed by a number to indicate pitch, and a second number to indicate duration. (See 'Suggestion(s) for extension'.)

Preparation

Set up a model 'delivery area' in the classroom, using cardboard boxes with numbers on to represent a sorting office, houses and shops. Make sure that the robot will have enough space to negotiate the route. Mark a collection of envelopes with appropriate addresses, including the

numbers of the cardboard houses. Prepare some arrow, number, 'Go' and 'Wait' cards (photocopiable pages 135 and 136 can be duplicated onto card for this purpose). Provide a bag or box for the letters; if possible, adapt the robot to resemble a postman.

Resources needed

A programmable floor or table robot (adapted to carry letters, if possible), boxes with numbers on to represent buildings, envelopes with appropriate addresses, a bag or box for delivering letters; arrow, number, 'Wait' and 'Go' cards (see 'Preparation').

What to do

In the context of work based on the local area, communication or shape and space, discuss the idea of having an automatic postal delivery service. With as much prompting as necessary, direct the discussion toward the idea of using a programmable robot for this. Remind the children of their previous experience of programming a floor robot and using cards to record the sequence of commands.

Ask for volunteers to program the robot to go from the 'sorting office' to two of the 'houses'. Remind all the children of the commands they have previously used. The volunteers will probably program the robot so that it will go to to the first house and continue without stopping until it reaches the second house, where it will stop. Ask the children for their comments, drawing out the need for the robot to stop at each house where it has post to deliver. Refer to the keyboard and ask the children whether they think any of the keys might be used to get the robot to wait. Once they have identified the 'Wait' key, demonstrate how to program the robot to wait for 10 seconds in between other actions (for example, *forward 2, right 1, forward 1, wait 10, back 1*). Ask for volunteers to enter similar sequences.

Now provide the letters in a suitable container; ask one

or two children to deliver post to two separate houses, starting from the sorting office and walking along a suitable route. Organise working groups of about three or four and set the task: to program the robot to deliver post. Devise a rota for the groups to work in succession. Select three letters for the first group to deliver; this group then selects three letters for the next group to deliver, and so on. The children should use programming cards, including the 'Wait' card, to plan and/or record their sequences of commands.

Suggestion(s) for extension

More confident children could experiment with the music key (if the robot has this facility). They could try pressing the key followed by two numbers. Can they say what the effect is of changing each number? (See 'Key background information'.)

Some children could try writing a sequence of commands to direct the robot from the classroom to the office or another suitable destination, and then test it.

Suggestion(s) for support

Try to make sure that less confident children work with more confident ones; if possible, provide adult support. Simplify the initial delivery route if appropriate, perhaps specifying only one address for delivery.

Assessment opportunities

Note whether the children use the 'Wait' key appropriately. Look for those who adopt a systematic approach, using the minimum number of commands necessary to complete the delivery sequence.

Display ideas

If there is enough space, an interactive display could be set up, inviting children to program the robot to visit various points in a model town or village.

Reference to photocopiable sheets

Photocopiable pages 135 and 136 have sample command cards (including 'Wait'), which can be duplicated for this activity.

SQUARE DANCE

To program a floor or table robot using the 'Repeat' command. To use a robot with the drawing device attached.

✝✝ *Whole class and groups of 3 or 4.*

🕐 *15 minutes discussion/demonstration time; 20–30 minutes for programming activity; 10 minutes for drawing activity.*

Previous skills/knowledge needed

The children should have some experience of entering commands into a floor robot and recording sequences with arrow and number cards.

Key background information

See 'Robot walk' on page 96 for general notes on the use of a programmable floor or table robot.

This activity introduces the 'Repeat' command, which is used widely in computer programming. For example, *Repeat 4 [right 1] Go* would result in a 360° turn. The repeat command is always followed by the number of times the sequence within the brackets should be carried out. This is extremely useful when programming the floor robot to draw regular polygons. Of course, if the degree of turn has been configured so that *right/left 1* means *right/left 90°* (as is recommended for work at Key Stage 1), squares or rectangles are the only shapes which can be programmed in this way.

Language to be introduced

Repeat.

Preparation

Prepare some 'Repeat' and open/close bracket ([and]) cards. Photocopiable pages 135 and 136 can be duplicated for this purpose. Some published cards use the same card ([ ]) for both opening and closing brackets. The command *repeat* is often written as RE or R. The cards you provide should have the appropriate letters or symbols for the particular robot that is being used.

Practise using the floor robot with the drawing device attached.

Resources needed

A programmable floor robot with a pen attachment device, large (A0 or A1) sheets of paper or card, adhesive tape or masking tape; arrow, number, 'Go', 'Repeat' and bracket cards (see photocopiable sheets 135 and 136).

What to do

Remind the children of their previous experiences of programming the floor robot and using the cards to record the sequence of commands. Ask for volunteers to program the robot to move around a square route and return to its starting position. Arrange the cards in sequence:

forward 1, right 1, forward 1, right 1, forward 1, right 1, forward 1, right 1, Go.

Ask the children whether they notice anything about this sequence. Once they have seen that *forward 1, right 1* is used four times, introduce the idea of repeating commands without having to enter them each time. Show them how the square program can be shortened to

repeat 4 [forward 1, right 1] Go,

pointing out the use of the number 4 and the use of brackets to contain the instruction or short sequence which is to be repeated.

Organise working groups of about three or four and set the task: to program the floor robot to move around a square. Give out the various command cards for them to use in planning and recording their commands. Devise a rota for them to carry out the task.

After every group has successfully completed the task, introduce the drawing device. (Each type of floor robot has a slightly different pen attachment device to allow its

INFORMATION
TECHNOLOGY

movements to be marked on paper.) Place a large sheet of paper on the floor or table (it may need to be held down at the corners with adhesive tape) and demonstrate how the robot can record its journeys. Provide opportunities for each group to practise using the robot with the pen attachment, producing squares or rectangles of different sizes on large sheets of paper.

Suggestion(s) for extension

Some children could be asked to program the robot to draw a pattern using squares, such as:

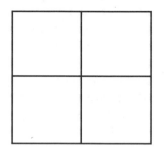

Suggestion(s) for support

Try to make sure that the less confident children work with those who are more confident with the task; if possible, provide additional adult support. You may find it helpful to explain the 'Repeat' command initially by repeating the single command *forward 1* and then repeating *right 1*, before repeating the two together.

Assessment opportunities

This activity incorporates all of the concepts and skills which have been introduced in previous control technology activities. It could be used to make a summative assessment of each child's attainment and progress in this area of IT. An adult helper will be needed if this is done – either to assist with monitoring and recording or to supervise other activities while you carry out the assessment with a group.

Display ideas

The different-sized squares drawn by the robot's pen could

be cut out and mounted alongside the command sequences.

Reference to photocopiable sheet

Photocopiable pages 135 and 136 have sample command cards (including 'Repeat'), which can be duplicated for this activity.

PROCEDURES

To program a floor or table robot using procedures.
†† Whole class and groups of 3.
🕒 *15 minutes discussion/demonstration time; 20–30 minutes activity time.*

Previous skills/knowledge needed

The children should have experience of entering commands into a floor robot and recording sequences with arrow and number cards. They should have used the 'Repeat' command.

Key background information

See 'Square dance' on page 102. The 'Repeat' command can be used to reduce the number of individual commands in a sequence; but it is also possible to save sets of commands and include them in later sequences. For example, if a square had been drawn with a screen turtle (see 'Screen square dance' on page 106) using the sequence *Repeat 4 [forward 1, right 90] End*, this could be given a name such as *square1* and saved for future use. Subsequently, the command *square1* would produce a square on the screen. As a name cannot be entered into a floor robots, each *procedure* is given a number and the prefix *P*. For example, when entering a procedure for drawing a square into a Roamer, the following sequence might be used:

P 1 [R 4 [F1, R1]]

The sequence of commands within a procedure is enclosed in square brackets. As the sequence for the repeat command is also enclosed in square brackets, this may look somewhat confusing. However, if children are confident in using the 'Repeat' command, they can usually

Figure 3

see the logic behind the procedure routine.

As long as the Roamer stays switched on, the procedure P1 will now remain in its memory. Thus the following short sequence will produce a square each time it is used:

P 1 Go

The Roamer can hold up to 99 different procedures in its memory. Once the *P* has been pressed, the beep which sounds as keys are pressed changes to a higher pitch until all the commands have been entered (indicated by the final] key press).

This activity assumes that a Roamer type of floor robot (see Figure 3) is being used. The commands for other floor robots are very similar, so the activity can easily be adapted for different robots.

Language to be introduced
Procedure.

Preparation
In addition to the range of cards required for previous activities, cards with the letter P are needed for this activity. Photocopiable page 136 can be duplicated onto card for this purpose.

Resources needed
A programmable floor robot with a pen attachment, large (A0 or A1) sheets of paper or card, adhesive tape or masking tape; arrow, number, 'Go', 'Repeat', bracket and 'Procedure' cards (see photocopiable sheets 135 and 136).

What to do
Remind the children of their previous experience of programming the floor robot and using the cards to record the sequence of commands. In particular, revise the use of the 'Repeat' key. Ask for volunteers to program the robot to move around a square; encourage the children to pay close attention to what is done, and particularly which keys are entered.

Tell the children that it is possible to save a sequence of commands for future use, reducing the number of commands which will have to be keyed in. If they were using a computer, they could give this sequence a name in the same way that they have already saved text files and

given them a name. However, the floor robot cannot accept names, so we have to number the sequences we want to save. Introduce the word *procedure*; write it on the board, and ask the children to practise saying it. Ask them whether they can spot a key on the robot which might have to do with procedures, making sure that they all eventually locate the *P* key on the control panel.

Use the cards to set out the sequence of commands for drawing a square:

R 4 [F1, R1]

Introduce the P card and tell the children that you are going to save the sequence as procedure number 1, then add a 1 card to make **P 1**. Now explain that, like repeats, procedures have to be enclosed in brackets; set out the cards in the order **P 1 [ ]**, leaving a space between the square brackets. Ask the children to suggest what should go inside the square brackets, drawing attention (if necessary) to the other sequence of cards: **R 4 [F1, R1]**. Ask for volunteers to place the first sequence of cards inside the square brackets, and talk the children through the new command sequence (see 'Key background information' above).

With the children's help, enter this sequence into the robot. Ask them to listen to the tone of the 'beep' as each separate key is pressed. Can they hear a change in the tone? Ask individual children to try out the procedure by keying in **P 1 Go**.

Organise the children into groups of three and devise a rota for them to practise entering procedures into the robot. Ask each group to devise a procedure which will make the robot draw a different-sized square. (They may need to stick the paper down using adhesive tape.) Assign each group a number for their procedure, and remind them not to switch off the machine until you ask them to do so. When it is their turn, they can key in earlier procedure numbers in order to see what other groups have done.

After all the groups have successfully carried out the task, they could (if time permits) attach the drawing device to record the robot's movements in each procedure. (See 'Square dance' on page 102.)

Suggestion(s) for extension

More confident children could be asked to program the robot to carry out consecutive procedures – for example, **P 1 P 4 Go**. They could also try adding other commands to a sequence including procedures – for example, **P 2 forward 2 P 3 right 4 Go**.

Suggestion(s) for support

Try to make sure that less confident children work together with more confident ones. Check that they are able to use the 'Repeat' command properly before asking them to use procedures. If it's possible, provide adult support.

Assessment opportunities

Children who carry out this task successfully, with a high degree of independence, will be attaining well above the national expectation for Key Stage 1. There is no agreed hierarchy for the development of skills in control technology, but the sequence of activities in this chapter reflects a progression from introductory work to tasks which are appropriate to Key Stage 2. They could also be used as in-service training activities for teachers who are unfamiliar with this area of IT.

This activity incorporates all of the concepts and skills which have been introduced in previous work on control technology. It could thus be used to make a summative assessment of each child's attainment and progress. Adult help will be needed, either to assist with monitoring and recording or to supervise other activities while the teacher carries out the assessment with a group.

Display ideas

The squares and other shapes drawn by the robot's pen could be cut out and mounted alongside the command sequences.

Reference to photocopiable sheet

Photocopiable pages 135 and 136 have sample command cards (including 'Procedure'), which can be duplicated for this activity.

TURN TURTLE

To program a screen turtle using commands familiar from work with floor robots.

†† *Whole class and pairs or groups of 3.*

⏱ *20 minutes discussion/demonstration time; 20–30 minutes activity time.*

Previous skills/knowledge needed

The children should have experience of using a floor robot. They should be familiar with the conventional commands such as *forward*, *backward*, *right* and *left*.

Key background information

Activities involving the movement of a marker around a screen are known as turtle graphics or turtle geometry. The reason for the use of the word *turtle* in this context is uncertain, but it may have arisen because the marker originally used on the screen looked something like a turtle. Many programs actually use a picture of a turtle as the marker, and many allow the user to choose from a range of images such as cars, planes and domestic animals. Turtle geometry is part of an approach to computer programming with the generic name of Logo. Proponents of Logo argue that it allows children to interact more easily with the computer by using commands and routines which are closely linked to everyday language. Although Logo is not mentioned specifically in the National Curriculum for IT, the kind of logical programming language that it involves is highly relevant to activities in control and modelling at all four key stages. At Key Stage 1, activities in turtle geometry provide opportunities for children to 'give direct signals or commands that produce a variety of outcomes, and describe the effects of their outcomes' (PoS statement 3b).

Different turtle geometry programs vary slightly in the way that commands are entered. For example, for *forward*, keying in *fo* may produce the whole word on the screen. Some programs have an on-screen control panel which is

operated with the mouse, replicating almost exactly the control panel of a floor turtle.

When children have become used to regarding a right angle as 1 unit of turn, they need to be introduced to the idea of turns being made in degrees. However, at this level they do not need to understand the meaning of '90°' fully (as being one quarter of 360°). Most children accept 90 and 180 as 'special numbers', and this is sufficient for them to carry out introductory activities with screen turtles. However, this activity provides valuable experience in preparation for mathematical work at Key Stage 2 or Scottish Levels C–E.

Preparation

It is important that you become familiar with the particular program you intend to use before introducing it to the children.

Resources needed

A computer with a turtle geometry program.

Language to be introduced

Screen turtle.

What to do

Remind the children of their previous work with the floor robot, and introduce them to the 'screen turtle'. Drawing on their existing knowledge of programming language, ask them to suggest commands for moving the turtle around the screen. Draw attention to the unit of movement, which may be a millimetre (depending on the particular program being used). Suggest moving the turtle in steps of 10 units (for example, 20, 30 and 40), and see the effect of moving forward by these distances on the screen. Introduce the use of *right/left 90* as an equivalent command to *right/left 1* in their previous work with the floor robot.

Organise the children into pairs or threes and devise a rota for them to practise using the program. They should take turns at entering commands on the screen and observing the results. No specific outcome is required; but the children may recall the sequence they used for drawing a square with the floor turtle, and try these out on the screen (this will successfully produce a square). Let the children discover for themselves how to transfer the Roamer commands to the screen environment.

Suggestion(s) for extension

Encourage more confident children to explore the program further, using repeat commands or drawing more complex patterns on the screen. See whether they can use the 'fill' command to colour in enclosed shapes.

Suggestion(s) for support

Try to provide some individual adult support for less confident children, or enlist the help of more confident children (perhaps acting as 'IT consultants') to provide guidance for them.

Assessment opportunities

Note the extent to which children transfer programming skills developed through activities with the floor robot to the screen environment. Look for children who are entering the correct commands independently.

Display ideas

A printout of the shapes and patterns produced by each child could be displayed, together with the command sequences used. If they have been 'filled' with colours on screen, the different shapes and patterns could be used as the basis of a collage (perhaps a 'turtle rockery') incorporating all the children's work .

SCREEN SQUARE DANCE

To build procedures using the 'Repeat' command.
To save procedures.

†† *Whole class and pairs or small groups.*

🕐 *20 minutes discussion/demonstration time; 30 minutes activity time.*

Previous skills/knowledge needed

The children should have basic experience of using turtle geometry, and of programming a floor or table robot.

Key background information

See 'Turn turtle' on page 105 for background material on turtle geometry. This activity involves saving *procedures*:

sequences of commands which produce a specific outcome. For example, a square with sides of one unit could be saved as a procedure called 'Square1', and this name could be incorporated into a subsequent sequence of commands (for example, to draw a house with square windows). Procedures in turtle geometry are similar to procedures in the programming of floor robots (see 'Procedures' on page 103), except that the former can be given names rather than numbers.

Language to be introduced
Sequence, procedure.

Preparation
The exact method for saving procedures will depend on the particular software being used. It is important to become familiar with this aspect of the program before introducing it to the children.

Resources needed
A computer with a turtle geometry program.

What to do
Remind the children of their work with the floor or table robot and with the current turtle geometry program, drawing particular attention to the use of the *repeat* command. Demonstrate how this is used on the screen. Instead of being put in brackets, the sequence to be repeated is often automatically indented after the command *repeat* is entered. The end of the repeat sequence is often signified by typing the word *end* or *next*.

Ask volunteers to try using the *repeat* command to draw squares of different sizes. Introduce the word 'procedure',

and ask the children to suggest names for the various sequences or procedures they have entered. These names should give an indication of what the procedure does. For example, *square3* would be appropriate for a procedure which drew a square with sides of 3cm; *rect42* would be appropriate for a rectangle with sides of 4cm and 2cm. Demonstrate how to name and save a procedure.

Organise the children into pairs or small groups and set the task: to create a square using the *repeat* command and to name and save this procedure. If time permits, the children could use their procedures to print patterns of squares. Set a time-limit for each group of 20 to 30 minutes, depending on the number of computers available.

Suggestion(s) for extension
More confident children could be encouraged to create more complex patterns based on squares, using the procedures they have saved and the *pen up/pen down* and *fill* commands.

Suggestion(s) for support
Depending on the program being used, less confident children may need help with saving the procedures. Try to provide adult or peer support.

Assessment opportunities
This activity involves a range of control skills, from basic techniques for directing the turtle to more advanced work using procedures. Careful monitoring of this activity could thus provide an assessment of each child's attainment and progress in control technology. Children completing the activity successfully and independently would be working above the level of capability expected at Key Stage 1.

APPENDIX: GENERIC PHOTOCOPIABLE SHEETS

Photocopiable pages 138 and 139 are intended for general use throughout the activities described in this book.

Photocopiable page 138: IT record sheet

Keeping track of children's individual attainment and progress in IT is difficult. It might be quite easy to assess their 'knowledge and understanding' through a paper test; but (especially at Key Stage 1) such methods have many inherent difficulties. If it is possible to spend sufficient time with individual children, observing them using the computer and other devices, it will be possible to assess their level of technical expertise; but IT is not simply about acquiring skills. While there is more emphasis on organising and analysing information at Key Stage 2, understanding should also be an issue at Key Stage 1.

So how can we assess both children's IT skills and their understanding of the subject? The first thing to consider is the use made of assessment. This is usually threefold: to find out what to teach next (formative assessment); to find out what children have learned at the end of a year (summative assessment); and to find out how effective a school is in teaching IT (evaluative assessment). From the class teacher's point of view, the first of these is perhaps the most important; but formative assessment normally feeds into summative and evaluative assessment.

In a busy class, the teacher has two main considerations: whether the children have covered a topic, used a particular program and so on; and how well they understand the processes and use the equipment. The former is much easier to assess, given appropriate organisation: a chart next to the computer with a simple tick list can provide a means of recording who has done what. Photocopiable page 138 takes this one step further, and has boxes indicating various levels of competence. This particular sheet is the one used for Key Stage 1 by Oaklands Primary School in Acocks Green, Birmingham. It is provided as an exemplar, and you may wish to customise it so that it fits more exactly with your planned IT activities.

It may be useful to ask children to complete this record with a partner. They can each have responsibility for checking – as far as they can – that the record is accurate. Each heading could be signed and dated by yourself or a classroom assistant when you have evidence that the record is accurate.

As you introduce each activity, point out the relevant heading on the record sheet. Being clear about what they are meant to learn from the activity will have a positive effect on the children's progress. Even very young children can appreciate that there is an underlying purpose behind work which, on the surface, simply provides enjoyable experience. The 'Assessment opportunities' section in each activity provides guidance about the assessment focus.

As more records are completed, it should be possible to identify children who need extra time on a particular activity. This can be more effective than responding to individual needs as they arise, and should lead to more efficient use of computer time. A statistical analysis of the records can provide an indication of the strengths and weaknesses in the children's understanding and technical skill, which might in turn be used to rethink teaching strategies and the emphasis given to particular aspects of the curriculum.

Photocopiable page 139: Saving your work

The more independently children can save and retrieve their computer work, the better. This needs some practise, but even very young children can be taught how to do it. It is not appropriate to map out a detailed progression for these skills: there is no obvious hierarchy, and many children would be frustrated if they were told 'We don't do that until Year 2'.

Photocopiable page 139 provides a step-by-step guide to saving work which applies to most programs in the PC format. This sheet can be made available near the computer, so that pupils – and adult assistants – can refer to it. To help younger children cope with the text, the key words can be highlighted (and other children can help).

Photocopiables

The pages in this section can be photocopied for use in the classroom or school which has purchased this book, and do not need to be declared in any return in respect of any photocopying licence.

They comprise a varied selection of both pupil and teacher resources, including pupil worksheets, resource material and record sheets to be completed by the teacher or children. Most of the photocopiable pages are related to individual activities in the book; the name of the activity is indicated at the top of the sheet, together with a page reference indicating where the lesson plan for that activity can be found.

Individual pages are discussed in detail within each lesson plan, accompanied by ideas for adaptation where appropriate – of course, each sheet can be adapted to suit your own needs and those of your class. Sheets can also be coloured, laminated, mounted on to card, enlarged and so on where appropriate.

Pupil worksheets and record sheets have spaces provided for children's names and for noting the date on which each sheet was used. This means that, if so required, they can be included easily within any pupil assessment portfolio.

INFORMATION
TECHNOLOGY

Title text, see page 19

Examples of text

Broadway

Snap

Providence

Ariel

Book Antiqua

Footlight

Brittanic Bold

Seagull

Wide Latin

Courier

Impress

INFORMAL

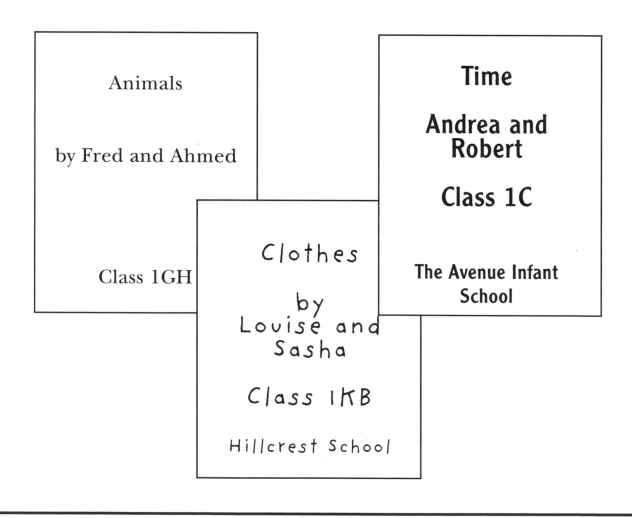

Animals

by Fred and Ahmed

Class 1GH

Clothes

by
Louise and
Sasha

Class 1KB

Hillcrest School

Time

**Andrea and
Robert**

Class 1C

**The Avenue Infant
School**

INFORMATION
TECHNOLOGY

What's on the menu? see page 22

Menu card

Starters

Chicken soup
Melon cocktail

Main Courses

Fish and chips
Burger and chips
Pizza

Desserts

Jelly and ice-cream
Banana split

INFORMATION
TECHNOLOGY

What's on the menu? see page 22

Table setting

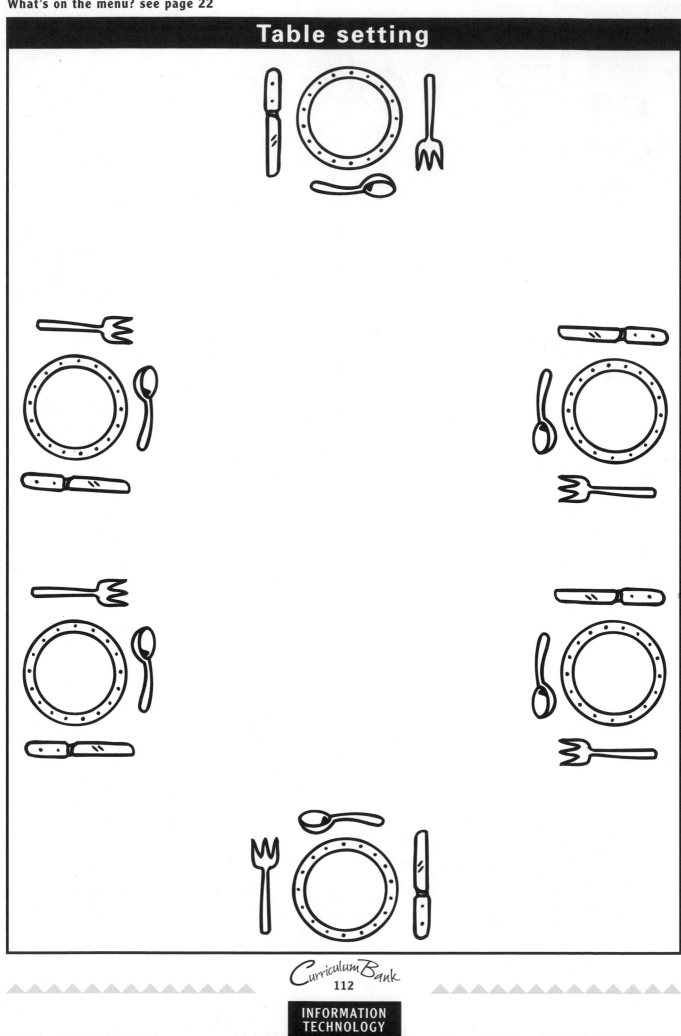

INFORMATION
TECHNOLOGY

Chef's special, see page 24

Recipe card

INFORMATION
TECHNOLOGY

Photocopiables

Dear Sir, see page 28

Examples of letter formats

The Willows School
Grange Road
Anytown
NE6 6JL

5th April, 1998

Dear Aunty Mabel,

Thank you very much …

With love from
Lucy

St Paul's CE School,
Villa Road,
New Town,
B22 5TT

May 22nd, 1998.

Dear Mr Jones,

We are doing a topic on …

Yours sincerely,
Robert Williams

King's Infant School,
Harbour Way,
Seatown,
AH1 4AD.

12th June, 1998.

Dear Miss James,

Thank you for coming to
visit our school yesterday …

Yours sincerely,
Nicola Marsh

Class 2b
Valley School

7.3.98

Dear Mrs Murphy,

We were sorry to hear you
were ill …

Get well soon!
Best wishes,
Dominic

INFORMATION
TECHNOLOGY

How it looks, see page 30

Class visits

Our visit to Legoland

North-East Buses

You can put your writing under the picture ...

The River Stour

or above it ...

High Fall Cliff

or
next
to
it ...

Borough Road Shops

Bakery

or
you
could

mix
them
up

Newsagent

INFORMATION
TECHNOLOGY

Who's who, see page 34

Teacher profile

Name _____ Class _____

How long have you been a teacher?

How long have you taught at this school?

What do you like about teaching here?

Do you have a favourite subject?

Which age group do you like teaching best?

Would you like to be a headteacher?

Why, or why not?

What do you like doing in your spare time?

News desk, see page 37

News office signs

EDITOR

NEWS DESK

SPORT

JOKES

ADVERTISING

SALES

INFORMATION
TECHNOLOGY

Take a pencil for a walk, see page 39

Walking the line

1. Choose a broad brush or thick crayon from the screen tools to draw a line with.

2. Draw a long line on the screen, making different shapes with it. Finish by joining the end of the line to the beginning.

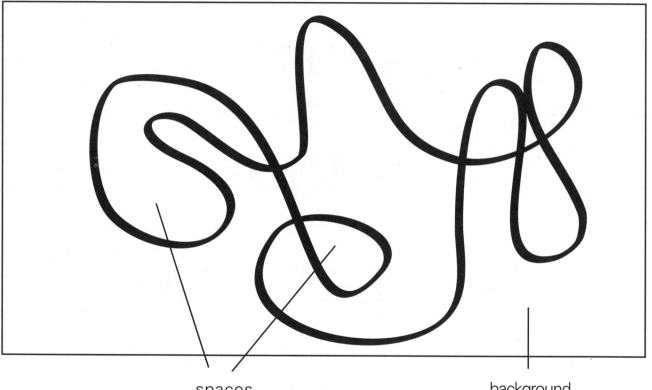

spaces   background

3. Choose the 'fill' tool and colour in a space. Select other colours to fill more spaces.

4. If you want to change a colour, just 'fill' the space again with a different colour.

5. Colour in the background using the 'fill' tool.

Photocopiables

Look, no scissors! see page 44

Wallpaper paste

1. Paint two flower heads. 'Cut' one out using the cutting tool. You can find this tool by selecting it from the toolbar. It might look like this:

2. Stamp the cut-out flower in a pattern on the screen. Leave spaces for the second flower.

3. Cut out the second flower. Use it to fill the spaces on the screen.

INFORMATION TECHNOLOGY

Underwater, see page 48

Computer help sheet

NOTE: Use this to put in details of your classroom computer.
Write step-by-step instructions on the 'screen'.

**INFORMATION
TECHNOLOGY**

Yes, that's me with the parachute, see page 54

Toolbox

This sheet is a guide to the drawing and painting tools used in graphics software programs. All such programs use **icons** to represent the tools available for drawing on the screen, changing colours, cutting and pasting, and so on. This means that skills learnt with one program can be used with another program. Whether you are using an Acorn system or a PC system, the drawing and painting tools should look quite similar.

Revellation 2 (Logotron) – a graphics program for Acorn systems

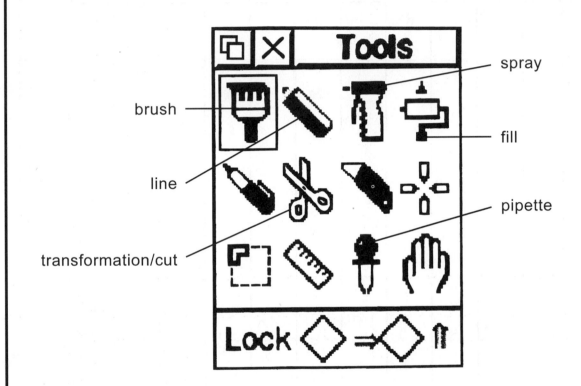

Colour Magic (RM plc) – a graphics program for PC systems

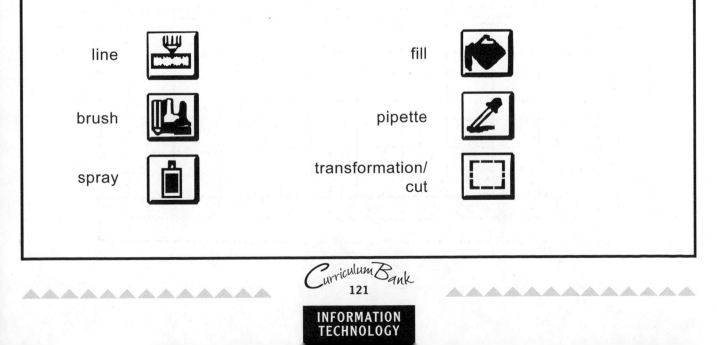

INFORMATION TECHNOLOGY

Traffic jam, see page 66

Traffic survey

Type of vehicle	Tally chart	Totals
Example: Cars	‖‖ ‖‖ ‖‖ ‖‖ |||	18

Start time ——— Finish time ——— Total time (mins) ———

Name(s) ———

INFORMATION TECHNOLOGY

Shampoo and set, see page 67

Hair colour survey

Hair colour	Tally chart	Totals
Example: Fair	|||| |||	8

Class

Name(s) _____

INFORMATION
TECHNOLOGY

Down at heel, see page 69

Shoe size survey

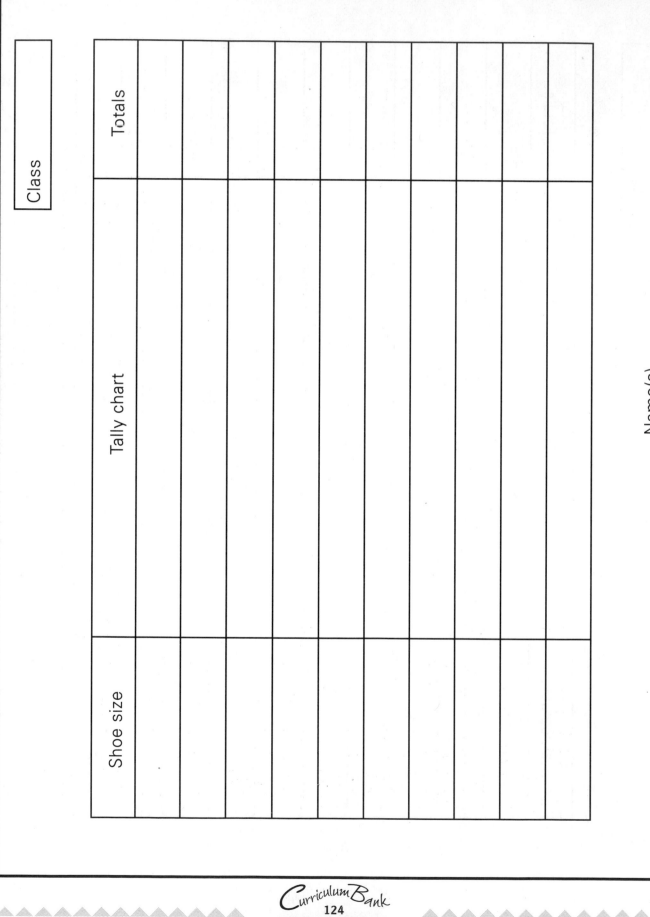

Class

Totals

Tally chart

Shoe size

Name(s) _____

**INFORMATION
TECHNOLOGY**

Bedtimes

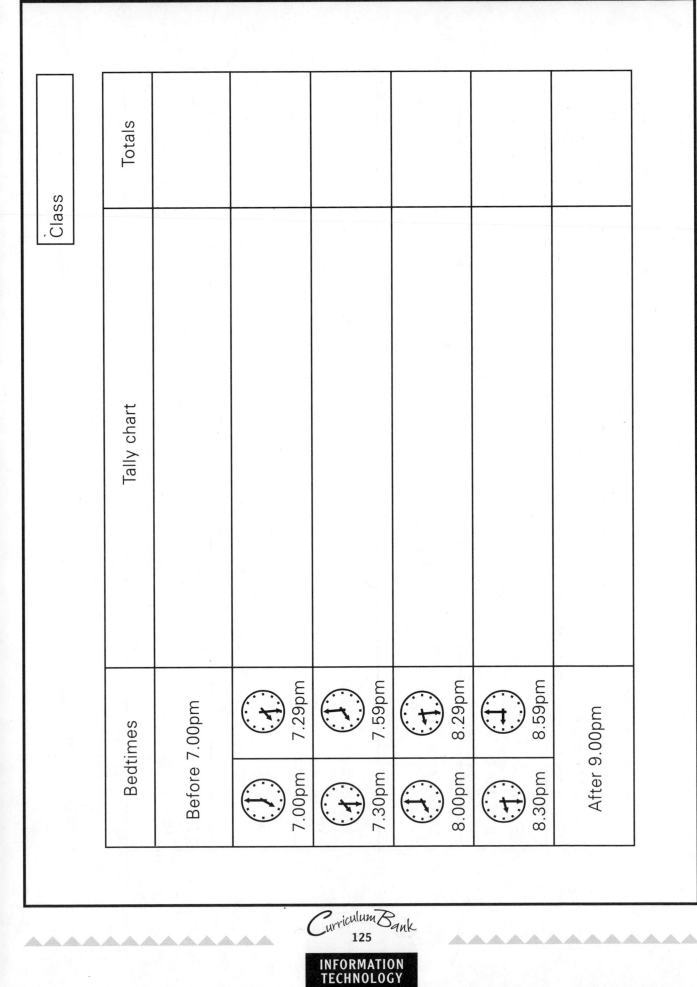

Class

Bedtimes	Tally chart	Totals
Before 7.00pm		
7.00pm — 7.29pm		
7.30pm — 7.59pm		
8.00pm — 8.29pm		
8.30pm — 8.59pm		
After 9.00pm		

INFORMATION TECHNOLOGY

Up the wooden hill, see page 70

Data handling record sheet

Name _____

Program _____

Record how well your partner can do the following things.

	no mistakes	some mistakes	a lot of mistakes
Enters information and makes	no mistakes	some mistakes	a lot of mistakes
Makes a bar chart with	no help	some help	a lot of help
Makes a pie diagram with	no help	some help	a lot of help
Saves the file with	no help	some help	a lot of help
Prints a graph with	no help	some help	a lot of help

Monitor's name _____

Date _____

INFORMATION
TECHNOLOGY

Discovery, see page 73

CD-ROM fact search

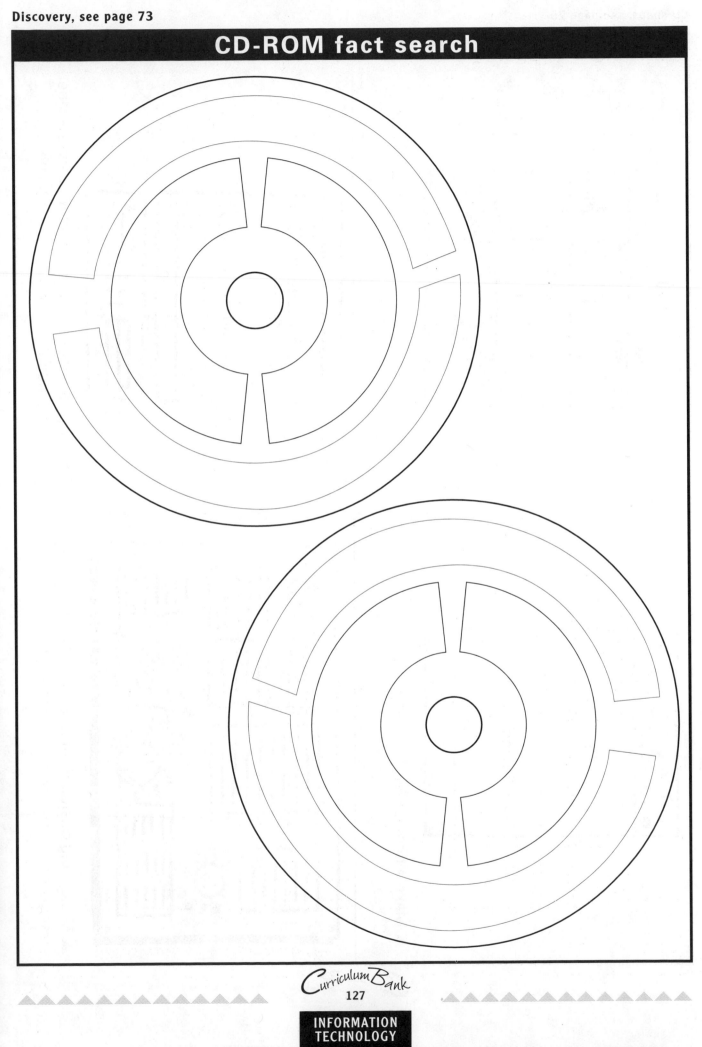

INFORMATION TECHNOLOGY

CD snaps, see page 75

CD-ROM fact show

▲ Make a book to hang up. Decorate the cover. Use the computer to make a label.

Minibeasts
Group 4

Minibeasts
Information
by Nadia and Felix

▲ Display your work on the computer. Make a label saying 'Come and see our work on Minibeasts'.

Minibeasts
by
Fred and Sonia

▲ Make a book cover that looks like a CD case.

▲ Make a big poster. Print out your work and arrange it on a large sheet of paper or card.

INFORMATION
TECHNOLOGY

Weather watch, see page 78

Weather record sheet

Monday	Tuesday	Wednesday	Thursday	Friday

Sunshine

cloudy *hazy* *sunny* *very sunny*

Rainfall

dry *drizzle* *showers* *rain* *hail* *snow*

Visibility

clear *mist* *fog* *pea-souper*

Temperature

freezing *chilly* *mild* *warm* *hot*

Temperature at 11.00am   2.00pm

Wind direction

NW   N   NE

W   E

SW   S   SE

Weather reporters

_____

_____

_____

Date _____

How does it feel? see page 79

Investigating materials

Name of material or object	Properties								

▲ Enter properties and/or materials as appropriate.

INFORMATION TECHNOLOGY

Photocopiables

Switched on, see page 86

Find the switches

▲ Can you spot the switches? Put a red circle around each one.

▲ Put a blue circle around each switch you spotted at home.

INFORMATION TECHNOLOGY

Turn it up, see page 88

Different kinds of switch

Name _____

▲ Draw each different kind of switch that you find. Underneath each picture, write what the switch controls.

INFORMATION TECHNOLOGY

In the picture, see page 89

Remote control unit

**INFORMATION
TECHNOLOGY**

Secret switches, see page 91

Supermarket switches

Name _____ Date _____

On the journey there:

At the doors:

In the electrical department:

In the frozen food department:

At the checkout:

INFORMATION
TECHNOLOGY

Direct a toy, see page 94

Arrow and number cards

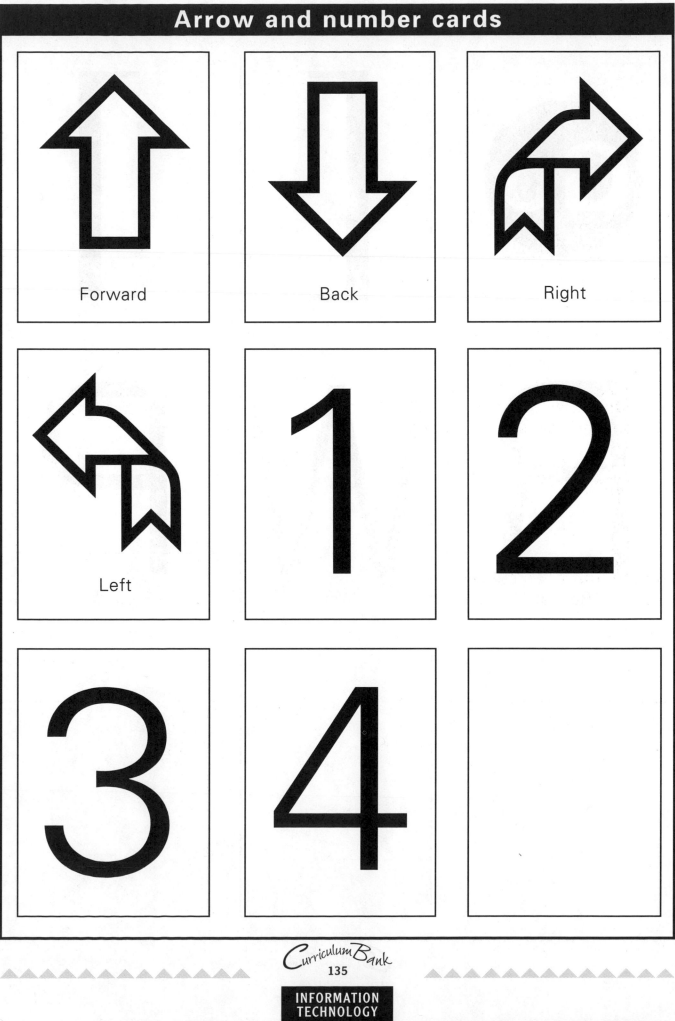

Forward

Back

Right

Left

1

2

3

4

INFORMATION TECHNOLOGY

Robot walk, see page 96

Command and bracket cards

Go

[

]

R
Repeat

W
Wait

P
Procedure

INFORMATION TECHNOLOGY

Robot walk, see page 96

The Roamer keyboard

▲ Write in the missing labels on this picture of a Roamer keyboard.

Forward

Cancel memory

Number keys

INFORMATION
TECHNOLOGY

See Appendix on page 108

IT record sheet

help others ☐ ☐☐☐☐ ☐☐☐☐ ☐ ☐ ☐ ☐

on my own ☐ ☐☐☐☐ ☐☐☐ ☐ ☐ ☐ ☐

in a group ☐ ☐☐☐☐ ☐☐☐ ☐ ☐ ☐ ☐

with help ☐☐☐☐ ☐☐☐ ☐ ☐ ☐

I can

Data handling

I collected some information.
I entered information into a database.
I produced a pictogram.
I produced a bar chart.
I produced a pie chart.
I made a simple search.

Control

I made a Roamer:
- move forward and backward
- turn left and right
- move to a location and return
- manoeuvre around obstacles
- play simple tunes.

Modelling

I can use a computer program to model a real situation.

Additional

I can describe how I work on the computer.
I can include sounds and music in my work using a computer.
I can compare IT with other ways of working.

---

help others ☐ ☐ ☐☐☐ ☐☐ ☐☐☐☐☐ ☐☐☐☐☐

on my own ☐ ☐ ☐☐☐ ☐☐ ☐☐☐☐☐ ☐☐☐☐☐

in a group ☐ ☐ ☐☐☐ ☐☐ ☐☐☐☐☐ ☐☐☐☐☐

with help ☐ ☐ ☐☐☐ ☐☐ ☐☐☐☐☐ ☐☐☐☐☐

I can

General skills

I can start a program from 'Windows'.
I can use a mouse to move objects on the screen.
I can use a mouse to choose from a menu.
I can use an overlay keyboard.
I can use a computer keyboard.

Word processing

Using a word processor, I can:
- type text
- move a cursor
- delete letters and words
- start a new line using the Enter key
- use upper and lower case letters
- save my work
- retrieve my work
- make changes to my work
- print my work.

Graphics program

Using a graphics program, I can:
- create patterns and pictures
- save my artwork
- retrieve my artwork
- make changes to my artwork
- print my artwork.

INFORMATION TECHNOLOGY

Saving your work

Saving a file

1. Think of a name for the piece of work you have done.
   Don't use your own name. Try to use a file name that reminds you what the work is about (for example, *Clocks*).

2. Once you have chosen a name, click on File.
   This gives you some choices.

3. The first time you save something, choose Save As. Now type in the name of your file (eg *Clocks*) and then click on Save.

4. The next time you save this work, just click on File and then Save.

5. Once the work has been saved, the name you have given it will be at the top of the screen.

Opening up a file you have already saved

1. Click on File and then Open.

2. You may not see your file name on the screen.
   If your work has been saved with other people's in a group of files or **directory**, you will have to open that group of files first. For example, if you opened a directory called *Time*, you might see the name of your file *Clocks*.

3. When you have found your file name, click on it and then click on Open or press *Enter* on the keyboard.

4. Don't forget to save your work again when you have finished.

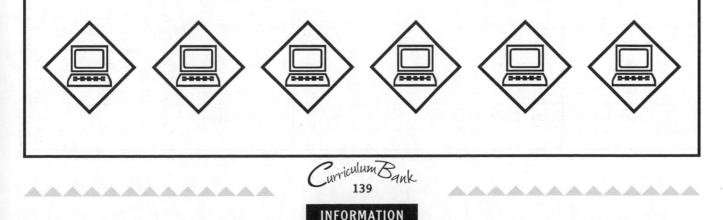

INFORMATION
TECHNOLOGY

Software

ACTIVITY	EXAMPLES OF SUITABLE SOFTWARE	
CHAPTER 1	**PC**	**ACORN**
Winter words	*Talking First Word, Creative Writer, Windows Concept, Clicker Plus, Textease*	*Concept Designer, Clicker Plus, Pendown, Textease*
Ice breaker	*Talking First Word, Creative Writer, Windows Concept, Clicker Plus, Textease*	*Concept Designer, Clicker Plus, Pendown, Textease*
This is me!	*Talking First Word, Creative Writer, Textease*	*Pendown, Textease*
Topical titles	*Talking First Word, Creative Writer, Textease*	*Pendown, Textease*
Filling the gaps	*Talking First Word, Creative Writer*	*Pendown, Folio, Textease*
What's on the menu?	*Talking First Word, Creative Writer, Textease*	*Pendown, Textease*
Chef's special	*Talking First Word, Creative Writer, Textease*	*Pendown*
Pen portraits	*Talking First Word, Creative Writer, Windows Concept, Clicker Plus, Textease*	*Concept Designer, Pendown, Textease, Clicker Plus*
Dear Sir	*First Word for Windows, Textease*	*Pendown, Textease*
How it looks	*Talking First Word, The Sherston Clip Art Collection, Bitfolio, Textease*	*Pendown, Textease, The Sherston Clip Art Collection, Bitfolio*
Short and sweet	*Talking First Word, Textease*	*Pendown, Textease*
The words that count	*Talking First Word, Textease*	*Pendown, Folio, Textease*
Who's who	*Talking First Word, Creative Writer, Windows Concept, Textease*	*Concept Designer, Pendown, Folio, Textease*
Wax lyrical	*Talking First Word, Textease*	*Pendown, Folio, Textease*
News desk	*Talking First Word, Colour Magic, Kidpix, Textease*	*Pendown, Pendown DTP, Folio, Textease, Kidpix, Splosh, 1st Paint, Revellation2*
Take a pencil for a walk	*Colour Magic, Kidpix*	*Kidpix, Splosh, Revellation2*
Stamp it out	*Colour Magic, Kidpix*	*Kidpix, Splosh, Revellation2*
Get into shape	*Colour Magic, Kidpix*	*Kidpix, Splosh, Colour Magic, Revellation2*
Look, no scissors!	*Colour Magic, Kidpix*	*Kidpix, Splosh, Colour Magic, Revellation2*
Colour swops	*Colour Magic, Kidpix*	*Kidpix, Splosh, Revellation2*
Planet of the shapes	*Colour Magic, Kidpix*	*Kidpix, Splosh, Revellation2*
Underwater	*Colour Magic, Kidpix*	*Kidpix, Splosh, Revellation2*
Light and shade	*Colour Magic, Kidpix*	*Kidpix, Splosh, Revellation2*
Spray that again!	*Colour Magic, Kidpix*	*Kidpix, Splosh, Revellation2*
Fearful symmetry	*Colour Magic, Kidpix*	*Kidpix, Splosh, Revellation2*
Yes, that's me with the parachute	*Junior Compose*	*Kidpix, Splosh, Revellation2*
Three blind mice	*Junior Compose*	*Compose World*
The teddy bears' picnic	*Junior Compose*	*Compose World*
If you're happy and you know it	*Junior Compose*	*Compose World*

INFORMATION TECHNOLOGY

Software

ACTIVITY	EXAMPLES OF SUITABLE SOFTWARE	
From major to minor	*Junior Compose*	*Compose World*
Join the band	*Junior Compose*	*Compose World*
CHAPTER 2	**PC**	**ACORN**
Six snakes, four ferrets	*Information Workshop, First Find It, Starting Graph*	*DataSweet3, Pictogram, Picturepoint*
Traffic jam	*Information Workshop, First Find It, Starting Graph*	*DataSweet3, Pictogram, Picturepoint*
Shampoo and set	*Information Workshop, First Find It, Starting Graph*	*DataSweet3, Pictogram, Picturepoint*
Down at heel	*Information Workshop, First Find It, Starting Graph*	*DataSweet3, Pictogram, Picturepoint*
Up the wooden hill	*Information Workshop, First Find It, Starting Graph*	*DataSweet3, Pictogram, Picturepoint*
Charting success	*Information Workshop, First Find It, Starting Graph*	*DataSweet3, Pictogram, Picturepoint*
Discovery	*Children's Encyclopedia*	*Kingfisher Children's Micropedia*
CD snaps	*Children's Encyclopedia*	*Kingfisher Children's Micropedia*
Weather watch	*Starting Grid*	*DataSweet3, Advantage*
How does it feel?	*Starting Grid*	*DataSweet3, Advantage*
CHAPTER 3	**PC**	**ACORN**
The bear essentials	*My World*	*My World*
That's life!	*My World*	*My World*
Switched on	No software is necessary	No software is necessary
Turn it up	No software is necessary	No software is necessary
In the picture	No software is necessary	No software is necessary
Secret switches	No software is necessary	No software is necessary
Direct a friend	No software or equipment is necessary	No software or equipment is necessary
Direct a toy	No software or equipment is necessary	No software or equipment is necessary
Robot walk	Roamer, Pip, Pixie	Roamer, Pip, Pixie
Slalom	Roamer, Pip, Pixie	Roamer, Pip, Pixie
Obstacle course	Roamer, Pip, Pixie	Roamer, Pip, Pixie
Robopostman	Roamer, Pip, Pixie	Roamer, Pip, Pixie
Square dance	Roamer, Pip, Pixie	Roamer, Pip, Pixie
Procedures	Roamer	Roamer
Turn turtle	*Roamer World, First Logo, SuperLogo*	*First Logo, Coco*
Screen square dance	*Roamer World, First Logo, SuperLogo*	*First Logo, Coco*

INFORMATION
TECHNOLOGY

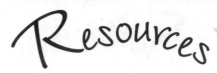

Resources

SOFTWARE	PUBLISHER	ADDRESS
1stPaint	Resource	Exeter Road, off Coventry Grove, Doncaster DN2 4PY
Advantage	RM: Research machines plc	New Mill House, 183 Milton Park, Abingdon, Oxfordshire OX14 4SE
Bitfolio	Logotron	124 Cambridge Science Park, Milton Road, Cambridge CB4 4ZS
Children's Encyclopedia (CD-ROM)	Dorling Kindersley	1 Horsham Gates, North Street, Horsham, West Sussex RH13 5PJ
Clicker Plus	Crick Software Ltd	1 The Avenue, Spinney Hill, Northampton NN3 6BA
Colour Magic	RM: Research machines plc	New Mill House, 183 Milton Park, Abingdon, Oxfordshire OX14 4SE
Compose World	ESP	75 Beechdale Road, Billborough, Nottinghamshire
Creative Writer	Microsoft	Microsoft Campus, Thames Valley Park, Reading RG6 1WJ
DataSweet3	Kudlian Soft	8a Nunhold Business Centre, Dark Lane, Hatton, Warks CV35 8XB
Information Workshop	RM: Research machines plc	New Mill House, 183 Milton Park, Abingdon, Oxfordshire OX14 4SE
Junior Compose	ESP	75 Beechdale Road, Billborough, Nottinghamshire
Kidpix	Broderbund	Allen House, Station Road, Egham, Surrey TW20 9NT
Kingfisher Children's Micropedia (CD-ROM)	Tag Development	25 Pelham Road, Gravesend, Kent DA11 0BR
My World	SEMERC	1 Broadbent Road, Oldham, OL1 4LB
PenDown	Logotron	124 Cambridge Science Park, Milton Road, Cambridge CB4 4ZS
Pictogram	Kudlian Soft	8a Nunhold Business Centre, Dark Lane, Hatton, Warks CV35 8XB
Picturepoint	Logotron	124 Cambridge Science Park, Milton Road, Cambridge CB4 4ZS
Revellation2	Logotron	124 Cambridge Science Park, Milton Road, Cambridge CB4 4ZS
Roamer World	RM: Research machines plc	New Mill House, 183 Milton Park, Abingdon, Oxfordshire OX14 4SE

INFORMATION TECHNOLOGY

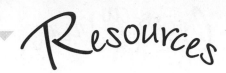

Splosh	Kudlian Soft	8a Nunhold Business Centre, Dark Lane, Hatton, Warks CV35 8XB
Starting Graph	RM: Research machines plc	New Mill House, 183 Milton Park, Abingdon, Oxfordshire OX14 4SE
Starting Grid	RM: Research machines plc	New Mill House, 183 Milton Park, Abingdon, Oxfordshire OX14 4SE
Talking First Word	RM: Research machines plc	New Mill House, 183 Milton Park, Abingdon, Oxfordshire OX14 4SE
Textease	Softease Limited	The Old Court House, St Peter's Church Yard, Derby DE1 1NN
The Sherston Clip Art Collection	Sherston Software Ltd	Angel House, Sherston, Malmesbury, Wiltshire, SN16 0LH
Windows Concept	RM: Research machines plc	New Mill House, 183 Milton Park, Abingdon, Oxfordshire OX14 4SE
EQUIPMENT	**SUPPLIER**	**ADDRESS**
Concept Keyboard, Keyboard 2000	The Concept Keyboard Company	9 The Murrills Estate, Porchester, Hampshire PO16 9RD
Universal Keyboard	Inclusive Technology	Saddleworth Business Park, Delph, Oldham OL3 5DF
Roamer, Roamer cards, pen pack	Valiant Technology	Valiant House, 3 Grange Mills, Weir Road, London SW12 0NE
Pip, Pixie	Swallow Systems	134 Cock Lane, High Wycombe, Buckinghamshire HP13 7EA

INFORMATION TECHNOLOGY

	ENGLISH	MATHS	SCIENCE	GEOGRAPHY	ART	MUSIC	D & T
Communicating information	Reading and writing text. Developing vocabulary. Identifying and correcting mistakes in text. Cloze procedure. Writing information text. Writing formal and informal letters. Drafting and redrafting a poem. Working on synonyms. Writing song lyrics. Writing 'newspaper' articles.			Using a school visit to observe and record characteristics of a location.	Selecting images from clip art to illustrate text. Drawing and colouring in a pattern on screen. Using the tools of a graphics software package to create representational and abstract images. Imitating artistic styles: Mondrian, Morris, Turner. Working with colours, shapes, silhouettes. Developing freehand drawing skills. Comparing the merits of screen and conventional drawing/painting methods.	Reproducing a musical sequence from individual phrases. Identifying the components and structure of a tune. Composing a tune from musical phrases, using key and tempo to create different moods. Using the computer alongside real instruments in performance.	Designing a menu card. Designing a recipe card. Producing a newspaper with photographs and text. Designing a wallpaper (or wrapping paper) pattern.
Handling information	Writing information text to explain numerical data. Reading and selecting passages of CD-ROM text to develop a theme.	Compiling and sorting numerical information, and displaying it in the form of a bar chart, pie chart or pictogram. Using a tally chart to record data. Choosing the most appropriate type of graph to present data. Making and recording measurements (eg of rainfall). Drawing Venn diagrams.	Being aware of the variety of pet animals in the domestic environment. Looking at variation within the class in terms of hair colour and shoe size. Examining materials to sort them according to their properties, using a range of criteria (including 'natural/artificial').	Looking at traffic levels in a particular location at different times. Observing the weather in the school location over a period of time.			Designing pages of information (text and pictures) selected from a CD-ROM.
Modelling and control	Giving directional instructions in oral and written form (including the use of symbols). Looking at icons as symbols which represent functions or instructions.	Understanding and using instructions which relate to position and movement: translation, rotation and repetition. Understanding angle as a measure of turn, eg that a right angle is a quarter-turn. Using repeated sequences to create patterns of squares and other shapes.	Being aware of practical reasons for clothing (warmth, protection). Looking at the life cycle of an animal (eg a frog or butterfly). Looking at electric/electronic switches at home, in school and in a supermarket; being aware that electronic switches can be triggered by movement, pressure, light or temperature.	Being aware of how weather or climate affects choice of clothing. Using directional commands to help a robot negotiate obstacles.	Creating patterns from repeated shapes.		

INFORMATION TECHNOLOGY